W9-ALJ-518

UNBORED
ADVENTURE

For the kids we grew up with, and their kids too.

UNBORED
ADVENTURE

70 SERIOUSLY FUN ACTIVITIES FOR KIDS & THEIR FAMILIES

JOSHUA GLENN & ELIZABETH FOY LARSEN

DESIGN BY TONY LEONE

ILLUSTRATIONS BY MISTER REUSCH & HEATHER KASUNICK

CHAPTER LETTERING BY CHRIS PIASCIK

B L O O M S B U R Y

NEW YORK · LONDON · OXFORD · NEW DELHI · SYDNEY

SOMERSET CO. LIBRARY
BRIDGEWATER, N.J. 08807

Our thanks to: Anton Mueller and the team at Bloomsbury; design assistant Cara Ciardelli; Lawry Hutcheson, who helped us build a box kite; and Kristin Gallagher at MindWare. We are particularly grateful to our children: Sam and Max Glenn; Peter, Henrik, and Luisa Schleisman; and Luciano and Luna Leone.

This book would not have been possible without the assistance of the following adventurers, young and old: Mauricio (Maui) Riedewald and Sam Knapp; Jonathan, Robin, and Junie Pinchera; Ena Nealon; Lila, Garet, and Emmett Glenn; Joshua Harrison; Luca, August, and Julian Gunther; Lily Devereux; Leela Moon Karlson; Riley Erben; Catherine and Patrick Hooley; Evan Barnes; Eddie Krasny; Henry Burton; Cesar Gallagher; Charlie Mitchell; Lauren Galle; Milo Waltenbaugh; Lisa Rosowsky; and Mark Frauenfelder.

BLOOMSBURY USA
An imprint of Bloomsbury Publishing Plc

1385 Broadway, New York, NY, 10018, USA
50 Bedford Square, London, WC1B 3DP, UK

www.bloomsbury.com

BLOOMSBURY and the Diana logo are trademarks of
Bloomsbury Publishing Plc

First published 2015

Copyright © 2015 by Joshua Glenn and Elizabeth Foy Larsen
Photographs © 2015 by Joshua Glenn and Elizabeth Foy
Larsen, unless otherwise noted
Illustrations © 2015 by Mister Reusch, as noted
Illustrations © 2015 by Heather Kasunick, as noted
Chapter divider and contents page illustrations
© 2015 by Chris Piascik

Some material appearing in this volume was previously published in slightly altered form in *Unbored: The Essential Field Guide to Serious Fun* (2012, US and UK editions).

All rights reserved. No part of this publication may be reproduced or transmitted in any form or by any means, electronic or mechanical, including photocopying, recording, or any information storage or retrieval system, without prior permission in writing from the publishers.

No responsibility for loss caused to any individual or organization acting on or refraining from action as a result of the material in this publication can be accepted by Bloomsbury or the author.

Published by Bloomsbury USA, New York
Bloomsbury is a trademark of Bloomsbury Publishing Plc

LIBRARY OF CONGRESS CATALOGING-IN-PUBLICATION
DATA HAS BEEN APPLIED FOR

ISBN: 978-1-63286-096-5

First U.S. edition 2015

1 3 5 7 9 10 8 6 4 2

Design and Art Direction by Tony Leone, Leone Design
Design assistance by Cara Ciardelli
Illustration illumination by Cara Ciardelli and Tony Leone
Cover design by Tony Leone
Cover illustration by Mister Reusch

For more activities and info, visit our website: Unbored.net

Printed and bound in China by RR Donnelley Asia Printing
Solutions Limited

To find out more about our authors and books visit
www.bloomsbury.com. Here you will find extracts, author
interviews, details of forthcoming events and the option
to sign up for our newsletters.

Bloomsbury books may be purchased for business or
promotional use. For information on bulk purchases
please contact Macmillan Corporate and Premium Sales
Department at specialmarkets@macmillan.com.

DISCLAIMER

The information contained in this book is for informational and entertainment purposes only. We have done our best to be as factual and accurate as possible, but we do not guarantee that any of the information contained in this book is correct or workable. Be responsible, exercise good sense, and take every safety precaution—not limited to the precautions that we suggest. Also, we do not advocate the breaking of any law.

Note that when following our instructions, switching materials, assembling improperly, mishandling, and misusing can cause harm; also, results may vary.

It is important that you understand that the authors, the publisher, and the bookseller cannot and will not guarantee your safety. Physical or mental harm is not intended so be cautious and use at your own risk. The authors and publishers expressly disclaim liability for any injury or damages resulting from the use (proper or otherwise) of any information in this book.

RECIPES, FORMULAS, ACTIVITIES, AND INSTRUCTIONS IN THIS BOOK SHOULD BE FOLLOWED EXACTLY AND SHOULD NOT BE ATTEMPTED WITHOUT ADULT SUPERVISION.

Because of the Children's Online Privacy Protection Act (COPPA), most major websites are restricted to users 13 and older. We do not advocate lying about your age in order to access websites, games, apps, social media services, and anything else online mentioned or not mentioned in this book. Parents should not help their children lie about their age online; if underage children make use of Facebook, YouTube, Twitter, Instagram, or any other website, game, app, or social media service, including web searches, they should only do so via a parent's account and with close parental supervision and collaboration.

While the authors have made every effort to provide accurate Internet addresses at the time of publication, neither the publisher nor the authors assume any responsibility for errors, or for changes that occur after publication. Further, the publisher does not have any control over and does not assume any responsibility for author or third-party websites or their content.

Chapter 1
ADVENTURE-IZE

Chapter 2

ADVENTURES CLOSE TO HOME

Chapter 3

URBAN ADVENTURE

Chapter 4

NATURE ADVENTURE

UNBORED'S
ADVENTURE
MANIFESTO

Illustration by Mister Reusch

Here's our Top 10 list of reasons for kids and grownups to take adventure seriously, whether it's on a mountaintop or in your own neighborhood.

1 Adventure motivates you to develop valuable skills and expertise, from building a fire and reading a map to repairing a bicycle or making friends with complete strangers.

2 Adventure challenges you to navigate your way through unfamiliar terrain… and also to see possibilities (even in familiar terrain, like your own home or backyard) for exploration and excitement.

3 Adventure rewards you for careful advance planning. And then, when things don't work out as you'd expected (they never do), it rewards you for adapting quickly and gracefully to the new circumstances.

4 Adventure teaches you to manage your fears, think rationally, ask good questions, and arrive at wise decisions—all in the space of a few moments.

5 Adventure is a game! One that you win by thinking on your feet, puzzling out the answers to difficult questions, and adapting as you go along.

6 Adventure yanks you out of your usual routine, offering you an opportunity to figure out what you're good at, what makes you tick, and what kind of person you want to be. It reveals the same about your friends, too.

7 Adventure demands that you share your know-how with and listen carefully to others, respect differences in your companions' ability and knowledge, and make crucial decisions democratically.

8 Adventure is a science! It's a process of trial and error, formulating hypotheses and testing them… and, above all, learning from your mistakes.

9 Adventure is an opportunity to escape from parental control, and do your own thing in your own way. You're on your own, responsible for yourself.

10 Adventurers are not only courageous, tough, and unflappable, but imaginative, unconventional, passionate, perceptive, and humorous. These character traits aren't just valuable when you're out on the trail, but in everyday life.

ADVENTURE-IZE!

By Chris Spurgeon

So you want to be an adventurer?

I've ridden a bicycle across America, tramped across England, and stood shivering in the middle of a swamp—at midnight—listening intently for the call of a rare bird. Big and small adventures like these have taught me several highly useful adventurer's habits and attitudes.

Keep it real

I once knew a wilderness skiing instructor who spent his winters in remote areas where, if something were to go wrong, there was no possibility of anyone coming to his rescue. So he understood that no matter how eager he might be to ski over a distant mountain, or plunge down a super-steep slope, it was very important that he make smart choices along the way.

Many wilderness accidents happen when intrepid but foolhardy adventurers psych themselves up to accomplish a goal that isn't doable in a safe way. So whenever he'd come to a potentially dangerous decision point, my friend

Illustration by Mister Reusch

would ask himself the following question: "If something goes wrong, can I get back to my car before dark?" The ultimate goal of an adventure should be to return home from it safely. If you should happen to accomplish something amazing between the time that you leave home and return, that's cool. But if you don't, that's cool too. There's always next time.

Build up your resilience

Depending on the type of adventure you're on, you might end up being hungry, thirsty, hot, cold, confused, miserable, angry, tired, anxious, maybe even scared. "But wait!" you say, "I thought adventures were supposed to be fun?" Here's the thing: Being uncomfortable and discontented is often the price of admission to the world of adventure. If you prefer always to remain perfectly comfortable and content, then the adventurer's life is not for you. However, I've learned from experience that the more adventures you have, the more resilient you get.

The first time you take a long hike and return home hours after dinnertime, you might feel like you're dying from exhaustion. But you won't die—and next time you hike, you'll remember that. It pays off to train ahead of time for big adventures: Taking short hikes and camping out in your backyard might not sound very exciting, but doing so will help get you accustomed to carrying a heavy pack and sleeping on the ground. Besides, training for an adventure can often turn into an adventure in itself; some people call this sort of thing a "micro-adventure."

Embrace failure

What makes an adventure an *adventure*? The possibility of failure, that's what. Having an adventure means that you might get temporarily lost, catch a cold, twist an ankle, or hate the weird food that you ordered. The key to any true adventure is risking just the right amount of failure—not too much, not too little. Neil Armstrong started off as a Boy Scout, a combat pilot in Korea, and an experimental test pilot; these experiences prepped him for his moon mission.

I've had adventures messed up by everything from the flu to broken airplane engines, to an injured knee to a lost passport… even forgetting to set my alarm. In the narrow sense that things didn't go precisely the way I'd planned, these adventures were failures. But when you're an adventurer, in the words of *MythBusters* host Adam Savage, "Failure is always an option!" In each of my "failed" adventures, overcoming difficulties became part of the fun.

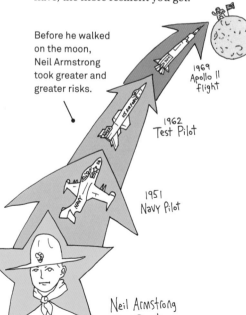

Before he walked on the moon, Neil Armstrong took greater and greater risks.

1969 Apollo II flight

1962 Test Pilot

1951 Navy Pilot

Neil Armstrong Boy Scout

TOP 10
ADVENTURE SKILLS

By Chris Spurgeon

Adventure is about taking risks! But the more prepared you are for those risks, the better. My kids and I have found certain adventure skills particularly helpful.

First Aid
Your local Red Cross and other organizations offer basic lifesaving classes. Take one!

Swimming
More than two-thirds of the Earth is covered with water. So knowing how to swim can literally be a matter of life and death. Besides, swimming is fun.

Open-mindedness
Your own culture is not automatically the best or most interesting one. Keeping an open mind is the first step towards one of the greatest adventures the world offers: travel to other lands.

Getting around
Want to expand your horizons the easy way? Learn how to navigate your town's bus or train system—and study the public transportation of any new city you visit.

Orienting yourself
Whether you're in a city or in the woods, study a map of the area and build up a mental picture of where things are located. You should be able to get back to where you started.

Don't panic
This advice comes from one of the greatest adventure novels, Douglas Adams's *The Hitchhiker's Guide to the Galaxy*. If something goes wrong, assess the situation calmly.

Expect the unexpected
A little part of your brain should always be thinking about what could go wrong, and what you'll do. For example: If my friends and I get separated, do we know where to meet up?

Solitude
For certain types of adventure, particularly in the wilderness, it's unsafe to travel alone. However, if you're too scared to try anything by yourself, then you'll limit your opportunities.

Sociability
On the other hand, it can be great to hike a while with people you've just met—or talk to those nice folks sitting at the next table in the café. Be wary of strangers, but don't be unfriendly.

Knowing your limits
The most important of all adventure skills, and the hardest to master. Experience will teach you how to know your limits. Until then, don't stress out about reaching some arbitrary goal.

Photos courtesy Tony Leone

BUILD AN ADVENTURE

CAMOUFLAGE YOURSELF

Where's Luciano? Thanks to his ghillie poncho, he's almost invisible.

By Tony Leone

Whether you're birdwatching in the woods or playing hide-and-seek with friends in a park, sometimes you need to conceal yourself. Short of acquiring an invisibility cloak, your best bet is to assemble your own ghillie poncho.

Designed to resemble heavy foliage, the ghillie suit was invented by Scottish gamekeepers for use when they were hunting deer and other game. (According to legend, the suit's name was borrowed from the *Ghillie Dhu*, a Scottish nature spirit garbed in leaves, moss, and twigs.) How does it work? By breaking up the wearer's human-shaped silhouette, so she blends into the surrounding scenery.

A full ghillie suit has arms and legs, and is very complicated to make. But fashioning a simple ghillie poncho will only take you and your grownup a couple of rainy afternoons.

You'll need:

- A 5'x7' piece of netting with about a 1" mesh. We used decorative netting from a Michaels arts and crafts store, repurposed from an actual fishing net. If your net smells fishy, let it air out for a day or two.
- 40' worth of 4"-wide burlap, in fall foliage colors. (Ghillie suits are too heavy and hot for summer use.) We used 20' worth of brown burlap, and 20' worth of olive-green burlap.
- 2' of yarn, in a "foliage" color.
- Sharp scissors, one pair per helper. Use with grownup supervision.
- Measuring tape
- **Optional:** Eye black, or charcoal

Prepare the camouflage

1. Using the scissors, and (as necessary) the measuring tape, cut up all of your burlap into strips of about 1" wide by 15"–18" long apiece. (Figures A & B)

2. Don't make the strips exactly alike! Their length and shape should vary.

3. Store the strips in a container until you're ready to put the suit together.

A

B

Prepare the netting poncho

1. Using the scissors, and (as necessary) the measuring tape, trim the netting until it's the proper size and shape to drape comfortably over your body. We trimmed ours to about 30"x60". Don't worry about cutting straight lines! (Figure C)

2. In the center of the netting, cut an opening large enough to fit your head through easily... but not so large that one of your shoulders will slip through the hole. (Figure D)

3. Thread the yarn around the head-opening's border. Tie the yarn's ends together. (Figure E)

Camouflage the poncho

Next, we're going to tie the burlap strips onto the netting poncho.

1. Before threading it into the netting, twist the end of each burlap strip. (Figure F)

2. Tie each strip with a simple knot, pulled tight. Some of the strips will fray and rip as you knot them, but that's OK! (Figures G & H)

3. If you're using multiple burlap colors, distribute the colors more or less evenly around the poncho—for maximum camouflage effect. Once you've attached about half the burlap strips to the netting, try it on and examine the coverage. Do you need more green on the shoulders? More brown along the edges? (Figure I)

4. Once you've used up all of the burlap, voilà! You've got a ghillie poncho. (Figure J)

➡ HACKS

- Camouflage any exposed skin, as necessary, with eye black or charcoal. (Figure K)

- You can tie any leftover netting around the top of your head, and thread bits of foliage—leaves, twigs, grass—into it. Or just wear a camo-colored hat or hood. (Figure L)

- Wear dark-colored or camo clothes under your ghillie poncho. (Figure M)

- Scope out a good perch—under trees, in a pile of leaves, or in a field of tall grass are all good spots.

- Keep quiet. While on the move, avoid stepping on twigs and dried leaves. You don't want to blow your cover!

ADVENTURE KIT
ESSENTIALS

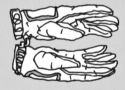

Whether you're heading downtown or to the top of a mountain, it's important to bring along the right gear. With the following items in your pack, we guarantee you'll make the most of your adventure... no matter what happens.

URBAN OUTINGS

Map and GPS
A smartphone with GPS is handy—but not always reliable. A laminated street map that includes landmarks such as museums and subway stations will help you navigate.

Sun protection
A brimmed hat, sunscreen, and sunglasses will protect your skin and eyes, and will help prevent dehydration. Don't forget lip balm with SPF.

Pocket change
If you should need to jump on a bus or train to get back home, a few dollars in change may come in handy. Find out how much a ride costs before you leave home.

Snacks
Nuts, trail mix, energy bars, or your favorite sandwich will keep your energy level high.

Water
To prevent dehydration, carry a water bottle—and refill it whenever you get the chance.

Charger
To recharge your phone or GPS device.

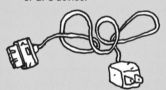

Extra clothing
Depending on the forecast, pack a hat, gloves, long or short-sleeved shirt, and rain gear.

Bag or sack
For picking up trash.

Illustration by Mister Reusch

NATURE OUTINGS

Topographic map
A topographic map not only shows trails, water, and other features of the terrain, it tells you how steep the hills are!

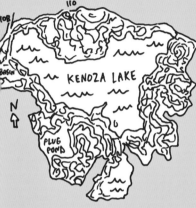

Compass
Essential if you get disoriented. Bonus: If your compass has a sighting mirror, you can flash it in the sun to show rescuers your location.

Food
Carry snacks and a day's worth of extra food—preferably something you don't have to cook.

Water
In addition to full water bottles, pack a water purifier or chemical treatment for lake or stream water.

Firestarters
Matches should either be fireproof or stored in a fireproof container. In addition to dry leaves and bark, clothes-dryer lint works well for tinder.

Pocket knife
Your knife—which you can use to fix gear, administer first aid, and make fire tinder—should have *at least* one foldout blade, a screwdriver, a can opener, and scissors.

Sun protection & first aid
In addition to sun protection, pack adhesive bandages, gauze pads and tape, over-the-counter pain relief, disinfecting ointment, and a topical antihistamine.

Extra clothing
In addition to the extra clothes you'd take on an urban adventure, bring along spare socks.

Toilet paper
Sure, you can wipe with leaves—as long as you stay away from poison ivy or poison oak. But biodegradable toilet paper is much more comfortable.

Light source
A headlamp or flashlight with LED bulbs is a must. Don't forget to pack spare batteries.

BE PREPARED!

AN EXCERPT FROM

GULLIVER'S TRAVELS

by Jonathan Swift

In the 19th century, Thomas Bowdler and his sister Henrietta published a children's edition of Shakespeare from which they'd deleted or altered all the offensive content. Since then, whenever a work of fiction has been altered and reissued in this manner, the new edition of the work (examples include Hugh Lofting's Doctor Dolittle books and Roald Dahl's *Charlie and the Chocolate Factory*) has been described—by outraged literature lovers—as "bowdlerized."

The following excerpt from Jonathan Swift's satirical 1726 novel *Gulliver's Travels* has not been included in many children's editions of the book. Washed up in Lilliput, a land of tiny people, the shipwrecked adventurer Gulliver becomes the honored guest of the emperor and empress. One night, there is a terrible fire. If you don't understand what's going on in this scene, perhaps we should explain that to "make water" or "void" means to pee.

PS: The Blefuscudians are another race of tiny people.

I was alarmed at midnight with the cries of many hundred people at my door; by which, being suddenly awaked, I was in some kind of terror. I heard the word *Burglum* [*Fire!*] repeated incessantly: several of the emperor's court, making their way through the crowd, entreated me to come immediately to the palace, where her imperial majesty's apartment was on fire, by the carelessness of a maid of honour, who fell asleep while she was reading a romance. I got up in an instant; and orders being given to clear the way before me, and it being likewise a moonshine night, I made a shift to get to the palace without trampling on any of the people. I found they had already applied ladders to the walls of the apartment, and were well provided with buckets, but the water was at some distance. These buckets were about the size of large thimbles, and the poor people supplied me with them as fast as they could: but the flame was so violent that they did little good. I might easily have stifled it with my coat, which I unfortunately left behind me for haste, and came away only in my leathern jerkin. The case seemed wholly desperate and deplorable; and this magnificent palace would have infallibly been burnt down to the ground, if, by a presence of mind unusual to me, I had not suddenly thought of an expedient. I had, the evening before, drunk plentifully of a most delicious wine called *glimigrim*, (the Blefuscudians call it *flunec*, but ours is esteemed the better sort,) which is very diuretic [*i.e., it makes you need to pee*]. By the luckiest chance in the world, I had not discharged myself of any part of it. The heat I had contracted by coming very near the flames, and by labouring to quench them, made the wine begin to operate by urine; which I voided in such a quantity, and applied so well to the proper places, that in three minutes the fire was wholly extinguished, and the rest of that noble pile, which had cost so many ages in erecting, preserved from destruction.

It was now day-light, and I returned to my house without waiting to congratulate with the emperor: because, although I had done a very eminent piece of service, yet I could not tell how his majesty might resent the manner by which I had performed it: for, by the fundamental laws of the realm, it is capital [*i.e., a serious criminal offense*] in any person, of what quality soever, to make water within the precincts of the palace. But I was a little comforted by a message from his majesty, "that he would give orders to the grand justiciary for passing my pardon in form," which, however, I could not obtain; and I was privately assured, "that the empress, conceiving the greatest abhorrence of what I had done, removed to the most distant side of the court, firmly resolved that those buildings should never be repaired for her use: and, in the presence of her chief confidents could not forbear vowing revenge."

BEST EVER

DYSTOPIAN ADVENTURES

Dystopian science fiction, which offers a glimpse of the terrible things that might happen if today's troubling social trends were permitted to develop and flourish, used to be written for grownups.

Since the 1960s, however, many great dystopian sci-fi novels have been written for kids. Here are a few favorites.

1963 (in English, 1964)

THE CITY UNDER GROUND

By Suzanne Martel
When a technologically advanced city-state, Surréal 3000, begins running out of energy, two sets of brothers explore its forbidden outskirts. There, they discover a forgotten secret about their city. Fans of Jeanne DuPrau's *City of Ember* might guess what it is. PS: This is the first sci-fi novel ever written by a Québécoise author.

1967–68 series

THE TRIPODS

By John Christopher
In *The White Mountains* (1967), Will and two other 13-year-olds join a resistance movement plotting against the alien invaders who've taken over the Earth. In *The City of Gold and Lead* (1968), Will infiltrates one of the Tripods' domed cities; and in *The Pool of Fire* (1968), he helps lead a planet-wide counter-attack against the Tripods.

Illustration by Mister Reusch

1973
THE ENDLESS PAVEMENT
By Jacqueline Jackson and William Perlmutter; illustrated by Richard Cuffari
Before *Wall-E*, this illustrated kids' book told the story of a girl named Josette, who drives everywhere in a personal "rollabout." Once upon a time, she discovers, people walked on their feet. Will she defy the Great Computermobile, and give walking a try?

1975
RANSOME REVISITED
By Elisabeth Mace
Years after a disaster has reduced British civilization to a primitive way of life, a girl discovers a copy of *Swallowdale*, one of Arthur Ransome's classic Swallows and Amazons adventure novels. Ransome's story gives her dangerous ideas about escaping from servitude… not to mention the tools to survive, once she does escape.

1978
A SWIFTLY TILTING PLANET
By Madeleine L'Engle
In this sequel to L'Engle's terrific books *A Wrinkle in Time* (1962) and *A Wind in the Door* (1973), the brilliant and perceptive Charles Wallace Murry must travel back in time in order to prevent a nuclear war. He is accompanied on his trip by a flying unicorn!

1980
THIS TIME OF DARKNESS
By H.M. Hoover
Eleven-year-old Amy has never set foot outside the massive domed city in which—ever since the Earth's environment was ruined—all of humankind has lived. When she meets Axel, a boy who claims he's from the Outside, the two attempt a daring getaway plan.

1983
WAITING FOR THE END OF THE WORLD
By Lee Harding
In a future Australia, young Manfred flees the polluted city for the countryside. There, he becomes aware that his medieval ancestors are offering him guidance on how to resist the powers that threaten him and his fellow refugees. But first, he must craft a longbow.

1990
ROCCO (a.k.a. A TIME OF DARKNESS)
By Sherryl Jordan
Rocco, a teenager transported forward in time to a primitive society of cave-dwellers, discovers that atomic war will obliterate modern civilization. Although he grows to love his new hunter-gatherer way of life, he must return to his own time and—somehow— prevent the war from ever taking place.

1998
OFF THE ROAD
By Nina Bawden
Ordered to report to a Memory Theme Park, because he's grown too old to be useful, Tom's grandfather flees from their perfectly regulated society. Following his grandfather into the scary wilderness, Tom discovers that their utopian society is actually… a dystopia.

2000
THE LAST BOOK IN THE UNIVERSE
By Rodman Philbrick
An orphan named "Spaz" crosses urban war zones— encountering the mutated gangs of each one along the way—in order to visit his dying sister. When he rescues a genetically improved girl, and visits her luxurious residential zone, he questions whether it's fair for one group of humans to live so well while others live in such squalor.

2014
PILLS AND STARSHIPS
By Lydia Millet
This moody "cli fi" (climate-oriented sci-fi) tale is set in Hawaii. While bidding farewell to their parents, Natalie and her brother Sam are recruited by a rebel organization that's dedicated to preserving what few animal species haven't already become extinct.

GET SET FOR
ADVENTURE

Q&A with Joshua Foer and Dylan Thuras

The user-written website Atlas Obscura (atlasobscura.com) aims to be an indispensable guide to the world's most "wondrous and curious places." So far, so good!

Since 2009, the site's contributors have chronicled everything from a flaming hole in the ground in Turkmenistan to the glowing millipedes of California's Sequoia National Park, to a precariously perched golden rock in Myanmar. We asked Atlas Obscura's co-founders for expert tips on getting yourself into the right mindset for an adventure.

UNBORED: What's the most crucial mental skill for a would-be adventurer to develop?

THURAS: You should practice cracking the codes of unfamiliar systems. You'll be confronted by them on adventures, whether you're deciphering a map written in an unfamiliar language, say, or figuring out a city's subway system. Puzzling out the solutions to real-world brainteasers offers a real sense of achievement.

Dylan Thuras (left) and Joshua Foer

UNBORED: Is it important for an adventurer to have particular equipment and tools?

FOER: I've recently lived with pygmies in the Congolese rainforest. Everything they use comes out of their surrounding environment. They've taught me that it's more important to learn to make do with what's at hand than it is to have a lot of fancy gear.

THURAS: That's true—but there's a lot to be said for having an adventure kit, whether that means heavy-duty survival gear or simply a notebook, pen, and rain jacket. The very act of assembling an adventure kit casts you in the role as a heroic adventurer, and can help make you more intrepid.

Photo courtesy Rob Dover

UNBORED: How do adventurers get motivated to move outside their comfort zones?

FOER: The best adventures are the ones where you find yourself right at the frontier of your comfort zone—not so far outside it that you're terrified, but far enough that you're excited. The more you push at that frontier, the larger your comfort zone grows. One way to expand your comfort zone is to meet people who don't share your perspective.

THURAS: Whether you travel halfway around the world or just a few blocks from home, one of the best ways to begin an adventure is to make a choice that you usually wouldn't make. Go into a place even if you don't need anything there; ask someone a question even if you don't need an answer. Do things without any "good" reason.

UNBORED: Does every adventure need to have a goal set in advance?

FOER: No! However, the best adventures often do start with a mission of some kind—perhaps you want to find out some information, or meet a particular person, or have a certain experience. Or you can just tell yourself, "I want to be able to tell a great story about this trip, later," and that desire can propel your adventure forward.

THURAS: Even if you're just wandering around your own neighborhood, you can assign yourself a mission… or some arbitrary rules, like: "I will turn left, and walk three blocks, then turn right and walk two blocks, and see what happens." Sometimes you'll end up somewhere that you think you're not supposed to be—but often it's just a lack of imagination that keeps us from exploring certain parts of our own familiar environment.

Illustration by Heather Kasunick

Want to get outside of your comfort zone? Assign yourself a mission!

Comfort zone

UNBORED: You two have been on expeditions together—including a trek checking out some of the hidden wonders of South America. What's the secret to good teamwork?

THURAS: Don't try to do everything on your own. Let your teammates use their skills.

FOER: Always trust your own intuition, but trust your teammates' intuitions as well.

UNBORED: When it comes to a successful adventure, how important is planning?

THURAS: You need a sense of where you're going, what you want to do there, how long it's going to take, what equipment you'll need, and so forth. Still, a big part of the fun is knowing that things won't go as planned—and embracing that.

FOER: Yes, when things are falling apart, treat that moment as part of the adventure. It's not an adventure unless there's a possibility of failure. That's the definition of adventure: "You don't know what the outcome is going to be."

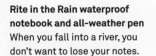

PACK
YOUR KIT

We asked Atlas Obscura's founders about the contents of their adventure kits.

Rite in the Rain waterproof notebook and all-weather pen
When you fall into a river, you don't want to lose your notes.

GPS Kit App (gpskit.garafa.com)
It's great for tracking where you've been and figuring out where you're going next.

Fanny pack
True, many people think these look ridiculous! But sometimes it's useful to have a camera, a notebook, and a Clif bar close at hand.

Sketchbook and Sakura Pigma Micron pen
Nothing helps you understand a place better than drawing it.

Small bag
For collecting weird rocks, ticket receipts, things people give you, and other mementos of an adventure.

Nalgene water bottle
They are indestructible.

Nuun electrolyte tablets
To help prevent yourself from becoming dehydrated and exhausted, drop two of these into your water bottle. Plus, they taste great.

GET DOWN,
MR. PRESIDENT!

Adventurers: 3 to 6

Playing an impromptu game is excellent training for would-be adventurers.

Why? Because if you want to win at them, you've got to learn to stay on your toes.

Try this:

1. When you're hanging around with friends or family members, discreetly and quietly put the pointer finger of your right hand to your right ear—as though you're a Secret Service agent who's just received a message.

2. As the members of your group notice what you're doing, they should also put their fingers to their ears. The last person to notice that the game has started, and therefore the last to put his finger to his ear, is automatically elected President.

3. As soon as the second-to-last member of the group joins the Secret Service, all the agents should yell, "Get down, Mr. President!" and then tackle the President to the ground. Gently! PS: The proper term of address, for a girl, is "Madame President."

➡ HACKS

- To prevent injury, your group can agree that, in each round of the game, only the first person to become a Secret Service agent is allowed to tackle the President.
- Email a photo of yourself (touching your ear, and perhaps wearing sunglasses) to a group of friends. All the members of the group must then send photos, to the entire group, of themselves doing the same thing. The last person to respond is automatically elected President and must tackle himself.

Illustration by Mister Reusch

FLOAT YOUR PANTS

& OTHER SURVIVAL SKILLS

The following scenarios are unlikely—but these survival skills are fun to practice. If you should find yourself in a situation where your practice pays off, then— you're welcome.

CAUTION! When practicing these survival skills, grownup supervision is a must.

FLOTATION PANTS

While out on the water, you temporarily remove your personal flotation device… and a freak wave pitches you into the drink. Luckily, you happen to be wearing a pair of pants.

You'll need:

- A pair of pants, worn over your bathing suit
- A body of water or swimming pool, and strong swimming skills. You should be able to tread water with just your legs for 10 minutes. However, you can also practice while standing up to your shoulders in the water.
- **Optional:** Flip flops, or footwear that it's OK to wear into the water

Illustrations by Mister Reusch

Use your legs to continuously tread water.

Try this:

1. Kick off your footwear, and then—while treading water—wriggle out of your pants.

2. While using your legs to tread water, knot the legs of your pants together. Make the knot as close to the foot holes as possible. Zip up the fly of your pants.

3. Put your head into the hole between your pants' legs, with the knot behind your neck.

4. Using both hands, grab each side of the pants' waistband. Pull it backwards over your head. Keeping a tight grip, lift the waistband of your pants above your head and then quickly yank the waistband forwards and down—towards the water in front of your face. This motion will shoot air into your pants' legs.

5. Quickly seal the waistband opening by squeezing it closed with your hands. Keep squeezing—the air inside your pants' legs should keep you afloat for a few minutes. Once the air seeps out, repeat Steps 4 and 5.

Be sure the knot is behind your head.

Hold the waistband tight to stay afloat as long as possible!

3. Spit onto the middle of one of the glasses' lenses, or drip some water onto the lens. Far-sighted glasses act like a magnifying glass, and a drop of liquid creates a more focused beam of light.

4. Hold the glasses a few inches above your pile of leaves, etc., and allow the sun's rays to shine through the lens with the liquid on it. A bright circle or dot will appear on the leaves—the smaller you can make this circle or dot, the hotter it will get.

5. Hold the beam very steady, and be patient. Once the leaves start smoking, gently blow on them until they burst into flames.

6. Enjoy your campfire, then extinguish it. Before you leave the area, feel the ashes with your hand to make sure they're completely cold.

MATCHLESS FIRE

One of your camping pals used the last match, but you need to get the campfire started. Luckily, you—or someone else in your group—is far-sighted, and is wearing glasses.

You'll need:

- A pair of far-sighted glasses
- Dry leaves, twigs, and/or newspaper
- A pail or bottle of water, to extinguish the fire
- An open outdoor area
- A sunny day
- Grownup supervision

Try this:

1. Prepare the campfire area by removing all dry grass and other debris. You might want to build a campfire circle of stones. Keep the water close at hand.

2. Gather the leaves, twigs, and/or newspaper into a small, fist-sized pile.

EMERGENCY CANDLE

A storm knocks out your home's power— but all your flashlights are dead. Luckily, this happened at breakfast time… and your family happened to have been frying bacon.

You'll need:

- Bacon grease. This activity is not for vegetarians, sorry.
- Small glass jar
- String
- A pencil or twig long enough to span the jar's mouth
- Scissors
- An outdoor space
- Grownup supervision, for the grease-collecting part

Try this:

1. Using the scissors, cut a piece of string that is as long as the jar is tall. (This is your candle's wick.) Tie one end of the string to the middle of the pencil or twig.

2. With a grownup's supervision, pour hot bacon grease into the jar. Be careful!

3. Before the grease begins to cool and solidify, lower the loose end of the string into the jar until the pencil or twig is resting on the jar's mouth.

4. Wait for the grease to harden completely. Note that you can speed up this process by putting your grease-filled jar part-way into cold water... or into a refrigerator, but of course in an emergency power outage you wouldn't be able to do the latter.

5. Once the grease hardens, cut the string off the pencil or twig, leaving about ½" of wick sticking out of the grease. Your candle is ready to use—outdoors, please. It's smelly!

NATURE'S SLEEPING BAG

While hiking, you get lost—and realize you'll have to spend the night outside. But you don't have a sleeping bag. Luckily, the ground is covered with leaves and brush.

You'll need:
- Dead leaves, grass, pine needles, or any other available debris

Try this:

1. Find a dry, level sleeping spot.

2. Gather all the debris you can find, and combine it into a pile that's longer than you are tall—and at least two feet high. Make sure you don't use any wet leaves or poison ivy.

3. Burrow into your natural sleeping bag and get some rest.

WHOₒₒₒₒ's in there?

Nighty-night! Don't let the chipmunks bite.

BUILD AN ADVENTURE

IMPROVISE A
BEAN-SHOOTER

If you've seen a Jackie Chan martial-arts movie, or any of the Pirates of the Caribbean movies, you know that sometimes an adventurer must fashion a tool or weapon from everyday objects.

Although we don't condone violence, we do enjoy shooting this bean-shooter—or gravel-shooter, or slingshot, or whatever you want to call it—at outdoor targets.

You'll need:

- A disposable plastic water bottle, empty and dry
- A latex or rubber glove; or a balloon
- A rubber band
- Scissors
- Dried beans; we used garbanzo beans
- Targets
- Safety goggles
- Open outdoor space

> **CAUTION!** Always wear safety goggles. Never shoot at a person.

Try this:

1. Remove the water bottle's cap. Using the scissors, carefully cut off the top 2" of the bottle. This removed section will look like a funnel. Recycle the bottle's bottom. (Figure A)

2. Using the scissors, cut off the thumb of the glove. If you're using a round balloon, knot the open end and then cut the knotted neck off the balloon's round part. If you're using a straight balloon, knot the open end, measure about 2" along the balloon, and cut. (Figure B)

Illustration by Heather Kasunick

3. Stretch the open end of the glove's thumb section (or the open end of the knotted balloon section) over the bottle's mouth. Pull the thumb or balloon section down around the ridges of the bottle's mouth, then secure it in place by tightly winding the rubber band around the lower half-inch of the thumb or balloon section. (Figure C)

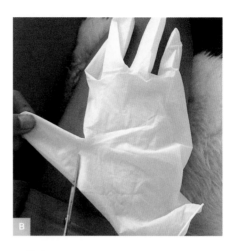

4. In your yard or another open outdoor space, set up targets—about 12 feet away from where you'll stand. Targets might include stuffed animals, moving wind-up toys, watering cans (which make a nice *ping* when you hit them), and empty plastic bottles. You can also draw bullseye targets on paper and tack them to a tree or fence.

5. Put on your goggles.

6. Place a bean inside the tip of the thumb (or balloon). Using your dominant hand, stretch back the rubber. Use your other hand to hold the bean-shooter steady.

7. Clear the target area of bystanders. Fire away!

⇒ H A C K S - - - - - - - - - - - -

Make a target shooting game by setting up four targets. Give each player four beans. On your turn, try to hit each target, scoring one point for each hit. Do this for three rounds—the player with the most points wins.

c.4th centuryAD
The first compasses were not designed for navigation! Using magnetic lodestones, Chinese spiritual guides invent a primitive compass to measure good and bad energy.

c.1st century AD
The Inuit people carve goggles out of walrus ivory, caribou antlers, and wood—to protect against snow blindness.

c.1500s
European hunters strap claw-like "grappettes" to the bottoms of their boots for traction on snow and ice. By the 1900s, these gadgets are known as "crampons."

------ Secret History of-- -

1609
The Italian astronomer Galileo invents an improved telescope. Eventually, Galileo's devices are so powerful they reveal the moon's craters.

c.1600s
Thanks to Galileo, various inventors get the idea to strap two telescopes together. Unlike the telescope, binoculars merge two views—producing an image with depth.

1803
Meriwether Lewis spends $2,324 on gear for his expedition through the Western US with William Clark. Among their supplies: 25 hatchets, 6 needles and silk ribbons.

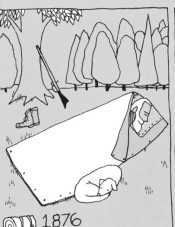

1876

A Welsh cloth merchant patents the "Euklisia Rug," a blanket that folds and fastens together, and which features a built-in pillow. It is the first mass-produced sleeping bag.

1891

Karl Elsener invents a folding pocket knife for the Swiss Army which features a screwdriver, a can opener, a leather punch, and an extra blade. It's still popular today.

1898

Ohio's National Carbon Co. introduces the first D cell battery—which paves the way for all kinds of battery-powered inventions, including the "electrical hand torch" or flashlight.

--Adventure Gear---

1920

While hiking in Alaska with an uncomfortable Inuit-made pack (sealskin stretched over sticks), Lloyd F. Nelson gets the idea for the first mass-produced external-frame pack.

1988

A cyclist and emergency medical technician fills an IV bag with water, puts it in his backpack, then sips through the bag's surgical tubing. This becomes the CamelBak.

1990

While bicycling, Gary Erickson bites into a tasteless energy bar and decides he can improve on the idea. He creates the CLIF bar in his mom's kitchen.

MAP
YOURSELF

Draw a large outline of your own head, then create a map of your brain inside it.

Maps don't have to be just for navigation. Using nothing more than your imagination and a few art supplies, you can express yourself by making a map of your own "personal geography"—that is, a map that captures the unique connection between you and a place.

You'll need:

- Art supplies—anything from paper to poster board or wood, from pencils to markers and paints, and from magazine cut-outs to stickers and photos. You can create images on a computer if you prefer.
- Don't forget school glue and scissors.

Getting started

Decide which place—it should be somewhere important to you—to map. Ideas from our first *Unbored* book include drawing a map of the inside of your home, from memory; or making a map showing your favorite (or least favorite) places in your town, state, or country. You might also try mapping, from memory, a place that you don't visit often: your kindergarten classroom, say, or your grandparents' home, or a town that you visit every summer.

Brainstorming exercise

If you can't immediately think of a particular location, make lists answering the following questions: What do I love to do? What do I hate? What are my favorite vacations, foods, hobbies, animals, friends? Many of the answers on your lists will have places associated with them— write those places down. Do any of these places capture your interest? Eureka!

Illustrations by Heather Kasunick

Shape and frame your creation

Maybe you're really into soccer—so make a world map in the shape of a soccer ball and fill it in with your favorite soccer teams from around the planet. Draw a frame around the edge of your map, or make a frame using strips of paper or cardboard, then decorate it. If you've made a map of a town where you vacation, then you might decorate the frame with drawings of objects that remind you of favorite vacation activities.

Creative re-use

You can repurpose an existing map—by personalizing it. On a road map of your state, draw pictures of places you've visited or would like to visit. Using a subway or bus map, rename all the stops based on what you like to do in that part of the city… or make up silly stop names.

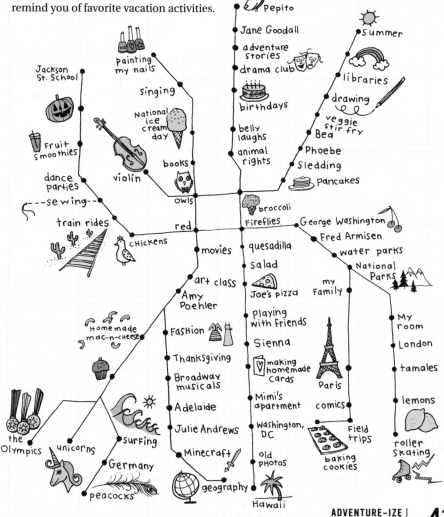

MAKE
THE CUT

Make sure you are following the knife safety rules.

Embarking on an outdoor adventure? A good, sharp knife is a crucial part of your equipment.

You can use a knife to slice an apple, spread peanut butter, cut sections of rope or string, even filet a fish. But the most fun thing to do with a knife is whittle a stick into a spear or an arrow. Never whittled? You can get started right in your home, by practicing on a bar of soap.

You'll need:

- A pocket knife—which should fold into a case, and lock into position when opened. Use with grownup supervision.
- A bar of soap
- A toothpick

> **CAUTION!** When using a knife, grownup supervision is a must.

Try this:

1. Unwrap the bar of soap and set it on a dry surface.

2. Using the toothpick, draw the shape you want to make on the bar of soap.

Illustration by Mister Reusch

3. Cutting away from yourself, and keeping your thumbs and fingers out of danger, carve away the parts of the soap that are outside the lines. Do this little by little, carving off small slivers, almost as if you were sharpening a pencil. If you cut off too much at once, the soap bar could break—and you could hurt yourself, too. Make every cut slow and controlled.

4. Once a rough version of your shape has emerged from the soap, use your knife to carve more exact edges. Don't worry about getting the soap's finish perfectly smooth, at this point.

5. Using the toothpick, add details to your sculpture's surface.

6. To create a smooth finish, rub the edges and surface of your sculpture with a wet finger.

KNIFE
SAFETY

DO
- Keep your knife closed except when you are using it.
- Cut away from yourself.

- Keep your blades sharp. A sharp blade is easier to control than a dull blade. You also won't use as much pressure with a sharp blade and therefore are less likely to slip.
- Keep your blades clean and dry—your knife will last longer.
- Close your knife before you pass it to someone else.

DON'T
- Carry your knife with the blade open.
- Throw your knife.
- Put your knife's blade into a flame. This can weaken the blade's strength.
- Use your knife's blade to dig.
- Pry something with the point of your knife's blade. It can snap off.

SHARPEN YOUR SENSES

Exercise your eye muscles!

Unlike purely physical traits, like the color of your eyes and hair, your senses can change! It all depends on how you train them.

As a would-be adventurer, it's important that you hone your senses until they're razor-sharp. Here are some exercises.

Sight

Do you spend a lot of time staring at screens? If so, then your eyes probably aren't getting enough exercise.

- Improve your depth perception (your ability to see how far things are from each other) by hiking in rough terrain—even if that just means leaping from rock to rock.

- Exercise your eye muscles by gazing at objects far away (clouds, mountains, even skyscrapers) and at tiny objects (grains of sand, flower petals, your own finger-prints). Test your eyesight by making exact drawings of all these objects.

- Sharpen your night vision by walking around (indoors or outdoors), attempting to identify the shapes surrounding you.

Touch

We often take our sense of touch for granted. Paying attention to how objects feel can stimulate your brain so that your sense of touch comes alive.

- Try stroking a soft object with your eyes open and closed. Notice any differences?

- With your eyes closed, remove objects from your family's junk drawer and organize them into categorized piles.

- Feel your clothes and then check the labels to see what they're made of. Can you tell the difference between fabrics?

- Hold a warm object in one hand, and a cold object in the other. Compare the sensations. Attempt to verbally describe the difference between the way these objects feel without using the words "warm," "cold," or their synonyms.

Illustrations by Heather Kasunick

Hearing

We rely so heavily on our vision that it's easy to forget how important hearing can be when you're on an adventure. Here are a few ways to give your ears a workout.

- With your eyes closed, walk around your house. With practice, you should be able to hear the difference between a closed-in space and a room with open doorways.

- Camp out in your backyard, and listen to the sounds of your neighborhood. You'll be surprised by how much activity you can hear: car doors slamming, footsteps, cats fighting, screen doors creaking...

- Listen to complex music—like classical, or jazz—with headphones on, at medium to low volume. Try to identify the sound of each individual instrument.

Improve your sense of smell!

Give your ears a workout!

Taste & Smell

Taste and smell are considered distinct senses, but they're interconnected—so these exercises are designed to help you develop both at the same time.

- Taste is maximized when we carefully look at and smell what we're eating. So inhale the aroma of what's on the end of your fork. Pay attention to how muddled the flavor of a stew or soup is compared to other dishes.

- Improve your sense of smell by closing your eyes and taking a whiff of various scents—spices, fruit, coffee beans, pencil shavings, grass cuttings, you name it. Make it quick, because your nose gets used to new odors and tunes them out.

SURVIVAL
ORIGAMI

Quench your thirst!
All you need is a
sheet of paper.

Adventurers are canny about making something they need, using whatever materials are at hand. You can create an origami cup in less than two minutes from an ordinary piece of paper.

You'll need:
• A sheet of 8 ½" x11" paper

Try this:

1. First, we'll need to turn the rectangular sheet of paper into a square. Holding the paper horizontally (that is, so the long edges become the rectangle's top and bottom sides), fold the bottom left of the rectangle up to the rectangle's top edge—creating a triangle.

2. Crease the leftover paper (that doesn't fit into the triangle) back and forth several times, then tear that strip off. Unfold the triangle: You now have a square sheet of paper.

3. Rotate the square until it's a diamond. Fold the bottom corner up to the top corner and flatten it out with your hand. You now have a triangle. (Figure A)

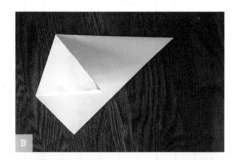

4. Pull the left corner up until its tip touches the top edge of the other side. Make a crease. Next, do the same with the right corner. (Figure B)

5. Now you'll have two flaps at the top of your soon-to-be cup. Pull the first flap down over the folds you made—but not all the way down; stop when there's about ¾" space remaining—and crease along the fold. Repeat this step on the other side of the cup, too. (Figure C)

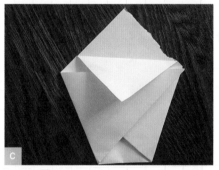

6. On each side of the cup's mouth, you should still have a flap that's approximately ¾" high. Fold these two flaps down, and crease along the fold—this will help the cup hold its shape. (Figure D)

7. Bottoms up! (Figure E)

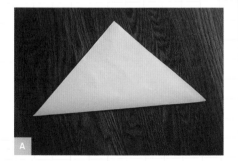

SURVIVAL ORIGAMI
VISUAL GUIDE

When it comes to folding, sometimes written instructions are confusing. Make a copy of this visual guide and take it along on your next adventure!

1

2 ✗

3

4

5

6

7

8

9

10

11

12

cup!

If you don't need your cup to drink with, use it for something fun.

Illustration by Heather Kasunick

ORIENT
YOURSELF

Use the sun's movement to orient yourself.

If you want to experience what it might be like to find your bearings and navigate without using a compass or GPS, here are a few fun challenges.

Navigating by night

Polaris, the North Star, sits directly over the North Pole; so if you're headed towards Polaris, you're headed North.

Try this:

1. Locate the Big Dipper, and trace its shape from the tip of its "handle" to the outermost side of its "cup."

2. The last two stars in the Big Dipper are known as "the Pointers," because if you draw an imaginary line between these stars and extend the line about four to five times that same distance, you'll discover that your line is pointing directly at the North Star. PS: Polaris is the brightest star in that region of the sky.

Navigating by day

At sunrise and sunset, it's easy to orient yourself via the sun, because—in the northern hemisphere, anyway—the sun rises in the east and sets in the west.

Try this:

1. On a sunny morning, find an open, flat area and drive a straight stick—about 3' long—vertically into the ground.

2. Place a pebble at the exact spot where the first shadow ends. Wait 20 minutes, while the shadow moves. Place a second pebble halfway up the shadow's new line. Draw a line between the two marks. What you've got now is a rough west/east line. A compass!

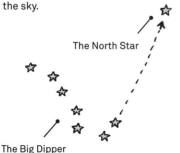

The North Star

The Big Dipper

Illustration by Mister Reusch

READY TO GO

Grownups really want kids to lead adventurous lives—but too often they assume that an adventure will happen if you "turn off the TV and go outside, already." It's not that simple!

Often, an adventure (like luck) is something that happens when preparation meets opportunity. There are always opportunities for adventure: weekends and vacations, snow days, spring and summer evenings. Unfortunately, you aren't always prepared for them. So train your grownup to help you be ready for adventure.

Illustration by Mister Reusch

Stockpile supplies

Work with your grownup to put together a comprehensive list of supplies that you'll need for all kinds of adventures. Depending on what you hope to do, your list might include some of the following items: backpacks or fanny packs, a multi-tool knife, compass and maps, heavyweight plastic tarps of various sizes, duct tape, 50-foot nylon cord, bungee cords, water bottles, first-aid kit, flashlight, extra flashlight batteries, waterproof containers, bicycle saddlebags, non-perishable food items, bicycle helmet, bicycle headlight, bicycle lock, bicycle patch-kit and tools, insect repellent and sunscreen, waterproof shoes and rain gear, a list of emergency contact numbers, binoculars, cash, and—last but not least—litter bags (for picking up trash).

Collect your adventure supplies and put them away until the time is right. A first-aid kid missing its band-aids, or a flashlight without batteries, isn't particularly useful on an adventure.

Maintain equipment

Your grownup can help—and teach—you to keep your adventure gear in proper working order. During the week, you might want to adjust the seat and handlebars of your bicycle, pump up the tires, and oil the chain so you can take off first thing on Saturday morning. If you have a pocketknife, keep the blade sharp. Test your flashlights' and bicycle lights' bulbs and batteries every so often. Check your boots to see if they're waterproof. Check packs and raincoats for rips and tears in the fabric, worn-out seams, and stuck or broken zippers.

Take test runs

How can you persuade your grownup that you're ready to explore on your own? Do a few adventure trips together. But ask them to allow you to be the leader. Ride your bikes to another part of town together, for example. Just remember to demonstrate that you're good at navigating, riding safely, and making good decisions. Ride in front of your grownup, and make signals before each turn. Stop at stop signs and red lights. Shout "Car back!" when a car is approaching from behind. Don't weave in and out of traffic or parked cars. Ride in a straight line, at a steady pace. Don't ride on the sidewalk. Walk your bike across busy streets.

Prove you can handle it

Before going on a family hike or car trip, ask if you can help plan, organize, and pack the supplies you'll need. When you return home from an adventure, don't just dump your gear in the garage: Take a few moments to wipe down a wet bicycle, coil a tangled rope, and put everything away where it belongs. If you've used anything up—batteries, say—then replenish.

Before a solo adventure, ask your grownup to make you a map showing how to get somewhere; and ask your grownup to describe landmarks that you should watch out for along the way. If you're carrying a mobile phone, make a test call before leaving. Reassure your grownup that you'll check in at a certain time, and then make sure you do.

ADVENTURES
CLOSE TO HOME

By Catherine Newman

Start your foraging career by picking wild berries.

Getting out of your comfort zone can be hard when you're, uh, in your comfort zone. That's why *The Odyssey* isn't just about Odysseus eating grilled–cheese sandwiches in his kitchen.

Still, if you approach your own house or apartment as a place to explore the unfamiliar, then you can have wild times galore. Start by walking in the front door backwards (seriously), to shake off whatever familiarness is clinging to your idea of home. Then let it get unboring.

Gather wild food

Foraging is the weirdly thrilling act of searching out and gathering edible plants and berries. This is definitely an activity with some risk involved!

But there are three ways to make foraging less risky. You'll want a great field guide, which you can likely get from the library; our current favorite is Ellen Zachos's *Backyard Foraging: 65 Familiar Plants You Didn't Know You Could Eat.* You'll want to be sure the area you're foraging in is clean, public, and free from

peeing dogs, pesticides, and pollution. And, finally, you'll want to be sure that you try only foods that have no poisonous look-a-likes; a good field guide should make this pretty obvious.

The best time to look for wild edibles in your backyard, neighborhood, or local park is spring. ("I could totally survive on wild foods!" my daughter Birdy, who is 12, likes to say. "As long as it was June!") But summer and fall are good too. And winter, if you live somewhere temperate.

Illustrations by Heather Kasunick

TOP 10 INSTANT ADVENTURES

By Catherine Newman

Conquer one fear
Watch a scary movie, read a book about spiders, learn self-defense, try asparagus.

Go outside at a different time from usual
Get up early to catch the sunrise, walk around your neighborhood after dinner, or go owling in the dark.

Get some citric acid
Mix it with water and baking soda and see what happens. Make sour candy or fizzing bath bombs.

Solve a mystery
Where are the pantry moths coming from? Why is the faucet leaking? How come the bread's getting moldy? If it's a problem, fix it.

Have an armchair adventure
Read *Owl Moon*, the Swallows and Amazons series, *Hatchet*, *My Side of the Mountain*, *Julie of the Wolves*, *Little House on the Prairie*, the Hardy Boys series.

Learn a skill
Ask someone who knows how to teach you to crochet, tie knots, count cards, whittle, paint a portrait, make an omelet, play the ukulele, build a bookcase, play chess.

Use a field guide
Identify fungi, birds, trees, clouds. Don't be shy about becoming an expert.

Hack your clothing
Make stencils from freezer paper, which you can get from the supermarket: Trace and cut out your design, iron the stencil shiny-side down onto your clothing, and paint with acrylic paint. Also: Turn a big shirt into a dress; turn a tee into a tank.

Look for four-leaf clovers
As Birdy likes to say: "Maybe the idea's that we have enough time to *look* for four-leaf clovers, and that's what makes finding them so lucky."

Keep an atlas on your coffee table
Or get a shower curtain with a map on it. When you're spacing out or lathering up, you can study the world.

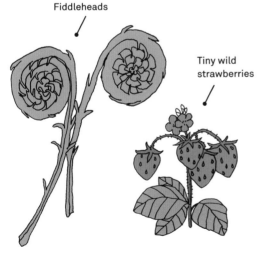

Fiddleheads

Tiny wild strawberries

Some great plants to start with, because they're safe and everywhere include: spring dandelion greens (make them into a salad with hot bacon and a vinegary dressing—yum); summer berries (tiny wild strawberries in a meadow, blackberries growing near the train tracks, blueberries up a mountainside); and fall nuts and seeds (black walnuts, which are complicated to deal with but worth it, and jewelweed seeds, which shoot out when you touch them, like the pods are miniature catapults). Cattails, milkweed, fiddlehead ferns, and violets all have edible parts too. I swear, you'll never look at weeds the same way again.

Experiment in the kitchen

Even if you're not foraging for bamboo and steaming its edible shoot (which I recommend), there is lots of adventure to be had with food. Think about the best or most exciting thing you've ever eaten and see if you can find a recipe for it: croissants, sushi, pot stickers, pickled turnips. You might need to stretch your skills, be patient, get help, or even mess up the first batch. And that's because this is the opposite of convenience food; think of it as *inconvenience* food, in a good way—a recipe that takes courage and then takes you to a faraway place.

You might try dabbling in "molecular gastronomy," which is a fancy way of describing edible science experiments. Do a web search for fizzing candy made from common supermarket ingredients. Pick up a kit that lets you make your own "popping boba", also known as "fruit caviar"; use it to "spherify" some Dr. Pepper, by mixing the soda with a seaweed-based thickener, then dripping it into a different chemical solution to make liquid-filled gel balls. Weird? Yes. Fun? Totally.

Unplug yourself

I don't just mean turning off the TV, putting down your phone for a minute, or skipping videogames for a night. I mean: Don't use any electric or battery-op anything at all, short of unplugging your fridge.

We've done this both deliberately, for a whole day, and inadvertently, for a whole week when our neighborhood had a massive power outage. We played board games by candlelight; we cooked sausages and biscuits on the woodstove; we made Jiffy Pop and played all our musical instruments and didn't shower; we lay on the living room floor, in the dark, and watched the snow fall past our windows. Short of actual time travel, there may be no better way to experience the adventurous side of everyday life.

Travel back in time! Unplug for a day.

You'll need smooth pavement and chalk to play these games.

Bring your own bottlecap!

BOTTLECAP
BATTLES

Adventurers: 2–5

During most of the 20th century, kids played games on the street or side-walk, or in a schoolyard or parking lot.

For each of these games, you'll need a safe and smooth area of pavement or cement, chalk, and modified bottlecaps known as "melties." With grownup supervision, melt candle wax (or crayons, if you like) into metal or plastic bottlecaps; you can also just stuff clay inside the caps. The extra weight will help your "melties" slide along the pavement more accurately.

Illustrations by Mister Reusch

LONDON CALLING

This game was originally known as "London." But we like the phrase "London Calling" because it's the title of one of our favorite punk records from the 1970s.

Try this:

1. Use chalk to draw a 3'x8' rectangle, then divide it into seven sections as shown in the illustration. Draw a semicircle on one end of the rectangle and write "LONDON" inside; this is the board's top.

2. On your turn, kneel at the board's bottom and—with a flick of your wrist—shoot your melty up the board. If your melty goes outside the board, or lands on a line, then your turn is over. If your melty lands inside a space, then begin drawing a stick-figure person, starting with a circle head, in that space. Write your initials inside the circle head.

3. On subsequent turns, if you land your melty in a space where you've already drawn a head, then add a body to it, then a leg, then another leg. If your melty lands in a space where you've already completed a chalk person, then start a new person next to it.

4. If your melty lands in London, then you may add a head to each of the seven spaces, *or* you can add a body part to the chalk people you've already started in each space.

5. If your melty lands in a space where you already have three completed people, then draw a line through them to represent linked arms. Were you the first to draw three linked people? If so, then you're the winner.

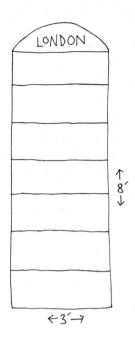

POTSY

Once upon a time, the game hopscotch was called "potsy." This hopscotch variant requires not only coordination, but quick thinking and a command of knowledge. Note that in addition to chalk and melties (for each player), you'll need a ball that bounces—a tennis ball, for example.

Try this:

1. Draw a line of 10 attached squares (each about 2'x2') along the ground. Write the name of a different category—for example, BIRD, CELEBRITY, HALLOWEEN COSTUME—in each square.

2. Mark a shooting line a reasonable distance away from the line of squares.

3. On your turn, kneel at the shooting line and shoot your melty onto the first square. If unsuccessful, your turn is over. If successful, you now "run the course," by bouncing the ball once into each square—and shouting an example of the category from the box in which the ball is currently bouncing. To use the examples above, you might shout, while bouncing the ball in these three boxes, "BLUE JAY! MILEY CYRUS! SKELETON!"

4. If you make an error—dropping the ball, for example, or bouncing it on a line or in the wrong box, or failing to name a correct example of a category before catching the ball—your turn ends. On your next turn, kneel at the shooting line and shoot your melty onto the square where you made your error. If unsuccessful, your turn is over. If successful, you now "run the course" again, beginning with that square.

5. If you're the first to finish the course, then you win.

ROCK BAND

COLOR

VILLAIN

TV SHOW

PIZZA TOPPING ↕ 20'

FOOTBALL TEAM

DONUT

HALLOWEEN COSTUME

CELEBRITY

BIRD

← 2' →

SKULLY

Also known as Skelly, Caps, and Dead Box, the game Skully has existed since the 1910s—which, not coincidentally, is when the crown-rimmed bottlecap was invented. You sometimes find old spray-painted Skully boards in schoolyards.

Try this:

1. Use the chalk to draw a large (approximately 5'x5') box on the pavement or cement. Within the box, draw 12 smaller boxes along the inside edge—see diagram. In any order, number the boxes 1 through 12. Draw a skull-and-crossbones in the center box. (Why? Because the center box is the "dead box.") Now you've got your Skully board.

2. Mark a shooting line a reasonable distance away from the Skully board.

3. On your turn, kneel at the shooting line and flick your melty at the square; on your first turn, you're attempting to slide the melty into the box marked 1. If you're successful, attempt to flick

MAKE A
MELTY

Once upon a time, kids carried melties with them everywhere—because you never knew when you might be invited to play a bottlecap game. Here's how to make one.

You'll need:
- A wax candle
- A bottlecap
- A protected work surface

Try this:

1. Light the candle. Grownup supervision is a must.

2. Drip the melting wax into the bottlecap. Don't overdo it! When the wax is level with the bottlecap's brim, you've created a melty.

3. Allow the wax to cool.

A flick of the wrist is all it takes to play.

Number the 12 small boxes in any order.

FLICK!

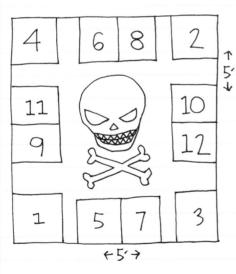

your melty from the shooting line into the box marked 2, then box 3, and so forth. If you miss a box, then it's the next player's turn. Note that your melty must end up entirely inside a box; if it lands on the line, or off the board, then your turn is over.

4. When it's your turn again, resume shooting for the box you missed on your previous turn. However, if last time your melty ended up on any part of the skull-and-crossbones, then you must start the game over at box 1.

5. If you're the first to finish the round by sliding your melty into box 12, then you win.

MONSTER!

Adventurers: The more the merrier

Here's a spooky–kooky indoor adventure game that is particularly fun to play at sleepovers.

Like Blind Man's Bluff, which combines elements of tag and hide-and-seek, Monster requires the player who's "It"—that's the Monster—to wear a blindfold. But everyone else is in the dark, too!

You'll need:
• A blindfold

Try this:

1. Agree on the game's boundaries, and remove breakable objects from harm's way.

2. Wait until dark, then turn off every single light in the house and pull down the curtains. Make sure it's as difficult to see as possible.

3. Switch on a light and gather around. Decide who will be the Monster and blindfold her.

Illustration by Mister Reusch

4. Switch out the light. Spin the Monster around five times. Everyone except the Monster should move around the perimeter of the room, while chanting something creepy, along these lines: "Monster, monster, come alive! Come alive at the count of five! One, two, three, four, five!"

5. The Monster moves around the room, stretching out her hands, trying to tag another player. Meanwhile, the players tease the Monster—trying to get as close to her as they can without being tagged. They're allowed to make noise.

6. Whenever a player is tagged, he must sit out the rest of the round. However, he can still make noises in an effort to confuse the Monster and get her to change direction. If you're the last player to be tagged, congratulations! You're the next Monster.

➡ HACKS

- In some versions of the game, whenever the Monster tags a player, she must feel that player's face. The tagged player is only eliminated if the Monster can identify him.
- You can make the game more hectic by giving the Monster a (soft) weapon, like a pillow or a Nerf sword. Before you do so, make sure that there's nothing breakable in the room.
- You can make the game more adventurous by expanding its boundaries to the entire house, or at least to multiple rooms. But don't let the Monster fall down the stairs.

KAGOME KAGOME

A less action-packed but equally creepy version of Monster is the Japanese game Kagome Kagome. Here's how it works. Choose one player to be the Monster; he sits in the center of the room, blindfolded. The other players form a circle around the Monster, join hands, then walk around and around, chanting: "Surround, surround, the Monster. Who-oo will take your place? Who-oo will take your place? Who-oo is standing behind you... NOW!" Everyone stops. If the Monster can guess which player is standing directly behind him, then that player becomes the new Monster. Otherwise, the game continues as before.

BEST EVER

SPOOKY HOUSE ADVENTURES

...TICK-TOCK...

Since the first century A.D., when Pliny the Younger related the legend of an unwary Greek philosopher's overnight stay in a haunted villa, spooky house adventure stories have thrilled and chilled us. Bumps in the night, strange lights, whispering voices... brrr!

You're probably familiar with recent classics of the genre, like R.L. Stine's *Welcome to Dead House*, Diana Wynne Jones's *Howl's Moving Castle*, and Neil Gaiman's *Coraline*. Not to mention famous examples like Edgar Allan Poe's *The Fall of the House of Usher* and Henry James's *The Turn of the Screw*. So here are a few of our favorite lesser-known spooky house adventures.

1954
THE CHILDREN OF GREEN KNOWE
By Lucy M. Boston
When he comes to live with his great-grandmother in her ancient house, young Tolly learns that the children who grew up there 300 years earlier are still around. This is the first in a series of six books, all of which the author set in her real-life home.

1958
MARIANNE DREAMS
By Catherine Storr
While ill in bed for weeks, 10-year-old Marianne draws pictures of a house, and a sad boy trapped inside. In a series of increasingly realistic dreams, she visits the house and befriends the boy. In order to help him out in real life, she must re-draw his entire world.

Illustration by Mister Reusch

1965
THE VELVET ROOM
By Zilpha Keatley Snyder
When Robin's migrant worker family moves to a boarded-up mansion near the ranch where they are working, a room full of books becomes a haven for her. But is the room haunted?

1968
THE HOUSE OF DIES DREAR
By Virginia Hamilton
Someone is prowling around an empty Ohio house that was once a station on the Underground Railway. Is it the ghost of Dies Drear, the house's former owner, and two murdered slaves? When an African-American family moves in, they must investigate.

1971
GOODY HALL
By Natalie Babbitt
Hired as a tutor in isolated Goody Hall, a Shakespeare-misquoting wanderer named Hercules Feltwright stumbles into an exciting adventure. This light-hearted tribute to the Gothic genre of fiction was written by the author of the popular novel *Tuck Everlasting*.

1973
THE HOUSE WITH A CLOCK IN ITS WALLS
By John Bellairs
Ten-year-old Lewis hears a clock ticking somewhere in the walls of his uncle's old stone mansion—which is full of secret passageways and unexplored rooms. Turns out that the house once belonged to an evil sorcerer… who's left behind a ticking doomsday device!

1974
THE PERILOUS GARD
By Elizabeth Marie Pope
Exiled to a remote English castle, Kate, a tomboy-ish lady-in-waiting for the future Queen Elizabeth II, learns that an ancient people known locally as the "Fairy Folk" dwells beneath it—underground. In order to rescue a stolen child, Kate must infiltrate the Fairy kingdom.

1983
BEHIND THE ATTIC WALL
By Sylvia Cassedy
Thrown out of boarding school for "poor adjustment," hard-hearted Maggie Turner winds up living with her great-aunts in the desolate, forbidding country house of her ancestors. Here, she discovers friends who teach her how to love. Too bad they're haunted dolls!

1987
MOONDIAL
By Helen Cresswell
When Minty, who has always been able to detect ghostly presences, stays with her godmother near Belton House, a 17th-century house in England's Lincolnshire county, she travels through time in order to release two childrens' spirits from bondage.

1988
SOMEPLACE STRANGE
By Ann Nocenti and John Bolton
Spike and Edward sneak into an abandoned house, where they discover a punk girl named Joy. The three are transported into a dimension where their attitudes—positive and negative—affect reality itself. A far-out comic reissued in 2014 as a graphic novel.

2005
TOYS IN THE BASEMENT
Written and illustrated by Stéphane Blanquet
A boy and girl wearing Halloween costumes are mistaken for toys and accidentally wind up in the secret underground lair of broken toys… who only want to get revenge on the children who've mistreated them. A freaky graphic novel translated into English in 2010.

2011
TUESDAYS AT THE CASTLE
By Jessica Day George
This book's first sentence says it all: "Whenever Castle Glower became bored, it would grow a new room or two." When the king and queen of Glower are assassinated and a foreign ruler attempts a coup, Princess Celie must defend the ever-shifting castle.

GO FLY A KITE

Bridle

Kite line

Sail

Sail

A 19th-century inventor built the first box kite; he hoped that his kite—which flew higher, and more stably than others—would lead to the development of a flying machine.

It did! Alberto Santos-Dumont was using the box-kite principle when he made history's first manned flight, in 1906. (The Wright Brothers' claim to fame is having invented the first controllable airplane.) You can start your own career as an adventurer the same way that these aeronautical pioneers did, by constructing a square-sectioned flying object that operates via aerodynamic lift... right at your own workbench or kitchen table.

We're very grateful to Lawry Hutcheson, for his box-kite expertise.

You'll need:

- At least 7 lengths of ⅛" x ⅛" x 24" basswood. Get extra lengths, in case of breakage.
- A ⅛" smooth-cut wood file
- A spool of ³⁄₁₆" gift ribbon, cut into 15 lengths, each at least 12" long.
- A large sheet of thin, flexible plastic fabric; we used a tall kitchen garbage bag.
- Cutting mat or board
- Measuring tape
- Marker
- A utility knife. Use with grownup supervision.
- Scissors
- Cellophane tape
- Clear packing tape
- A spool of kite line (20 lb. test)

Illustration by Heather Kasunick

Construct the box

A box kite is constructed of four long parallel struts; the box is made rigid with short crossed struts. We recommend constructing the box in the following manner. Do all filing and cutting on the cutting mat or board to avoid damaging your work surface.

1. Using the measuring tape and marker, make three marks on one of the lengths of basswood: Two of the marks should be ½" from either end; and the third in the center. Repeat this process on three more lengths of basswood. These are your *long parallel struts*. (Figure A)

2. Using the ⅛" wood file, carefully file grooves into the *long parallel struts* at each of the places you've marked. File about halfway through the wood, or a bit less, each time. (Figure B)

3. Now we'll make the *cross struts*. Mark the center point on three other lengths of basswood. Using the utility knife, saw each length of wood in half. On the top face of each of the half-lengths of wood, make two marks—each ½" from either end. Now rotate the wood so that its marked face is pointed down at your work surface. At the center of each of these half-lengths of wood, on the face now aimed directly at you, make a mark.

4. Using the ⅛" wood file, carefully file grooves into the *cross struts* at each of the places you've marked. File about halfway through the wood, or a bit less, each time.

5. Line up two of the *long struts*, with the grooves facing upwards. Place three of the *cross struts* on top of the long struts, in a perpendicular fashion; the outer grooves on each of the three cross struts should line up with the grooves on the two long struts. (Figure C)

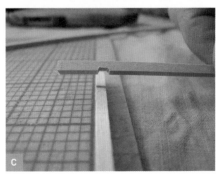

6. Using the lengths of gift ribbon you've cut, lash the long struts and cross struts together at each joint [see Lashing Knot sidebar].

7. Now place the remaining three cross struts perpendicularly on top of one of remaining long struts; the outer grooves on each of the three cross struts should line up with the grooves on the long strut. (Figure D)

8. Weave the finished and unfinished sections of the kite together, so that the grooves in the cross struts on the finished section are meshed with the grooves in the cross struts on the unfinished section. Lash the two sections' cross struts together at these three joints. (Figure E)

9. Finish up the second section by lashing its remaining long strut to its three cross struts.

LASHING KNOT

You might need a friend to help you hold the struts in place.

1. Place the short strut perpendicularly on top of the long strut; fit the grooves together. Slide the center of your length of gift ribbon underneath the long strut, then pull the ribbon's ends straight up on either side of the long strut—in front of the cross strut.

2. Pull the ribbon's ends forward, over the short strut. Cross the ribbon ends underneath the short strut, and pull tightly. (Figure A)

3. Bring the ribbon ends back over the top of the cross strut and towards yourself. Pull the ends straight down, then tie a half knot underneath the long strut. Pull the knot tight.

4. Pull the ribbon ends straight up on either side of the long strut—in front of the cross strut—and tie another half knot, above the long strut. Pull the knot tight. (Figure B)

5. Pass the ribbon ends underneath the short strut, then pull them up on either side of the long strut. Now tie a full knot, tightly. (Figure C)

6. Trim and/or curl the leftover ends of the ribbon as desired. (Figure D)

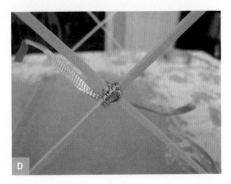

Add the sails

The width of each of the kite's two "sails" ought to be (individually) about ¼ or ⅓ of the length of the box. When we're done cutting the sails, we'll wrap them around either end of the box, leaving the ends and middle of the kite open.

1. Using the measuring tape and marker, mark two sails on your plastic fabric— each sail should be 36" long, and 6" or 7" wide. (Figure A & B) Note that if you're using a garbage bag, you should first deconstruct the bag by cutting along its seam and bottom edge.

2. Using the scissors, cut out the two sails. (Figure C) If the edges of your sails are a little ragged, that's OK. However, if the sails' edges are very ragged, then the kite may not fly well.

3. Tape one of the first sail's short edges to one of your kite's long struts, near— but not all the way at—the strut's end. Use cellophane tape first, and then once the sail is taped exactly the way you want it, reinforce the cellophane tape with packing tape. (Figure D)

4. Repeat Step 3 three times, until the first sail is completely attached. Use clear packing tape to fasten down the sail's remaining length. (Figure E)

5. Repeat Steps 3 and 4 for the second sail.

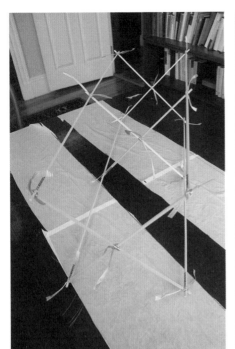

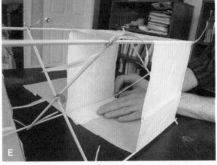

Attach the bridle

There are various theories about the best way to attach kite line to your box kite; note that whichever method you choose, the attachment is known as the kite's "bridle." You can experiment with your kite and line to achieve the best result, but here's one method.

1. Using the scissors, cut a 34" length of kite line. This is your bridle.

2. Knot one end of the bridle to one of your kite's long struts, near the outside edge of one of the sails. (Figure A)

3. Knot the other end of the bridle to the same strut, near the outside edge of the other sail. Use small pieces of packing tape to fasten the bridle ends in place.

4. Knot the free end of your spool of kite line to the center of your kite's bridle.

WHAT ARE THE ODDS?

INSTANT → ADVENTURE

Adventurers: 2

The dare-ee must respond to a dare by giving odds.

Daring a friend to do something she would prefer not to do? Meh. Challenging her to a game that will determine whether or not she *must* accept your dare? Now that's fun.

Here's how the game works.

The darer issues a dare to the dare-ee. Nothing too dangerous or disgusting, please. "What are the odds that you'll drink this cup of spaghetti sauce?" is a good one. So is "What are the odds that you'll stick your feet in this bucket of ice water for 20 seconds?"

The dare-ee *must* respond to this dare with odds between 1 and 250. If she really doesn't want to accept the dare, then she'll say something like "1 out of 247." However, if she's not bothered by the dare, then she might reply, say, "1 out of 14."

Only the dare-ee can name the odds! However, the darer can try to cajole the dare-ee into naming lower odds: "1 out of 176? Come on. How about 1 out of 99, at least?"

Once the odds have been agreed upon, the two players count down from 3: "3-2-1." At "1," the darer and the daree must each say a number from 1 up to the agreed-upon odds. If the odds were "1 out of 4," then the numbers 1, 2, 3, or 4 would all work.

If the players say the same number, then the darer wins the game… and the dare-ee must immediately perform the dare. In most cases, however, the players will say different numbers, and the game will end without a winner or loser. Until next time.

Here's a common variant rule: If a dare-ee refuses to give odds, then the odds are automatically 1 out of 15.

Illustration by Mister Reusch

ENGINEER A
PLAYBORHOOD

Q&A with Mike Lanza

When Mike Lanza started looking for a home for his family, he wanted a neighborhood where kids run around in packs, inventing stuff and playing games. Instead, he found neighborhoods where kids didn't play outdoors.

Together with his wife and three children, Lanza set out to transform their Menlo Park, Calif., neighborhood into a "playborhood." He chronicled their efforts on the blog Playborhood.com, and later wrote a smart, helpful book with the same title.

We asked Lanza what it takes to—in his words—"turn your neighborhood into a place for play."

UNBORED: Kids used to go outside and find their own fun and adventures. What's changed?

LANZA: When the playground was invented 100 years ago, it was because so many kids were playing on the streets that it bothered the people who were driving in cars. There's been a power struggle between children and grownups for a long time… and now grownups have won.

Mike Lanza and his family

UNBORED: Why can't grownups just kick kids outside?

LANZA: In order for a kid to have fun outside, they need to have other kids outside with them. Today, almost all neighborhoods are dead; kids aren't outside playing. We need to change that, so that kids will come outside and see it as the most fun thing they can do. If all you know is how to be driven around to activities or play videogames, you won't know what to do when you are outside. It's something you have to get in the habit of doing.

UNBORED: What can families do to turn their outside spaces into places where kids want to hang out?

Photo courtesy Nicole Scarborough

LANZA: Because kids have so many things they can do inside, those outside spaces need to be interesting and have a lot of fun things to do. Really little kids love to play with water and sand. Older kids love to climb and play with balls, build and hang out in forts and play games.

A kid's parents might think this will make the yard too messy. The question is: Do you want your yard to be neat, or a place for fun? If you take your things inside and put them back in the exact same place every day, it doesn't invite other kids to come over to play.

UNBORED: What's one easy step a neighborhood can take to turn itself into a playborhood?

LANZA: Don't play in the backyard. If you go in the front or side lot or the street, more people will see you and join in, and it will become contagious.

UNBORED: What can a kid say to grownups who worry that it's not safe for kids to go out and roam around by themselves?

LANZA: Tell them, "The numbers say that America is a safer place today than when you were kids." They can look up the crime rates if they don't believe you.

UNBORED: Does a kid's smartphone encourage or discourage adventure?

LANZA: A smartphone helps you figure out for yourself where to go and how to get home. A lot of kids are fantastic at navigating the videogame world… if you have a smartphone with a map app, you can navigate the real world better than grownups can! Also, having a phone makes it easy for kids and parents to call each other and check in.

Illustration by Mister Reusch

ADVENTURE IN YOUR OWN BACKYARD

AN EXCERPT FROM

THE WOULDBEGOODS

by E. Nesbit

One of the first children's authors whose stories combine contemporary settings with fantasy elements, Edith Nesbit has influenced everyone from *Mary Poppins* author P.L. Travers to J.K. Rowling. But Nesbit's characters don't need magical assistance to find adventure. In this scene from *The Wouldbegoods* (1901), Dora, Oswald, Dicky, and Alice Bastable decide to rescue a milk-pan that has fallen into the moat of a house where they're staying for the summer. With the help of their younger siblings Noel and H.O., and their less daring friends Daisy and Denny, they construct a raft from an old barn door and other scavenged materials.

We found some nice little tubs stuck up on the fence of the farm garden, and nobody seemed to want them for anything just then, so we took them. Denny had a box of tools someone had given him for his last birthday; they were rather rotten little things, but the gimlet worked all right, so we managed to make holes in the edges of the tubs and fasten them with string under the four corners of the old door. [...]

At last the gallant craft rode upon the waves. We manned her, though not up to our full strength, because if more than four got on the water came up too near our knees, and we feared she might founder if over-manned.

Daisy and Denny did not want to go on the raft, white mice that they were, so that was all right. And as H.O. had been wet through once he was not very keen. Alice promised Noel her best paint-brush if he'd give up and not go, because we knew well that the voyage was fraught with deep dangers, though the exact danger that lay in wait for us under the dairy window we never even thought of.

So we four elder ones got on the raft very carefully; and even then, every time we moved the water swished up over the raft and hid our feet. But I must say it was a jolly decent raft. […]

Then those on shore waved a fond adieu as well as they could with the dampness of their handkerchiefs, which we had had to use to dry our legs and feet when we put on our stockings for dinner, and slowly and stately the good ship moved away from shore, riding on the waves as though they were her native element.

We kept her going with the hop-poles, and we kept her steady in the same way, but we could not always keep her steady enough, and we could not always keep her in the wind's eye. That is to say, she went where we did not want, and once she bumped her corner against the barn wall, and all the crew had to sit down suddenly to avoid falling overboard into a watery grave. Of course then the waves swept her decks, and when we got up again we said that we should have to change completely before tea.

But we pressed on undaunted, and at last our saucy craft came into port, under the dairy window and there was the milk-pan, for whose sake we had endured such hardships and privations, standing up on its edge quite quietly.

The girls did not wait for orders from the captain, as they ought to have done; but they cried out, "Oh, here it is!" and then both reached out to get it. Anyone who has pursued a naval career will see that of course the raft capsized. For a moment it felt like standing on the roof of the house, and the next moment the ship stood up on end and shot the whole crew into the dark waters.

Plan to bury your capsule for at least 10 years.

MAKE & HIDE A
TIME CAPSULE

Time-travel adventures aren't possible. But by preserving the present in a time capsule, we can enable our future selves to travel backwards through time.

Capture aspects of your everyday life and world, and stash them somewhere where they won't be disturbed for years. Your future self will be grateful.

You'll need:

- A shoebox; or, if you're burying your time capsule, a large empty can or jar (with lid)
- Duct tape
- Stuff that you want to include in your time capsule. For example: paper and writing utensils of various colors, for making lists and drawings, or writing essays or poems; magazines and scissors; photographs; postcards; ribbon or string; all sorts of objects.
- Permanent marker
- Shovel, if you're burying your time capsule

Illustrations by Heather Kasunick

Try this:

1. Write an introductory note to the future you who opens this time capsule. Include your current age, your address, the name of your school, and your predictions and hopes about what you'll be doing in the future.

2. Make lots of lists. Here are some ideas: names of your family members, friends, schoolmates, pets; your favorite subjects in school; what you like to do when you aren't in school; favorite TV and YouTube shows, restaurants, slang words, musicians, authors. (Figure A) Roll the lists up with your introductory note, and tie the scroll with a ribbon or string.

3. Add ephemera. This might include: pictures cut out of magazines, showing not only who today's celebrities are but how people dress and what cars look like; a postcard showing what your city or town looks like now; photos of your family and friends; the front page of today's newspaper, or a printout from your family's favorite news website; small objects of any sort—but nothing that will rot, decay, or leak!

4. Put the lid on, and seal your time capsule with duct tape. If you're planning to bury your capsule, then you might want to completely wrap it in duct tape. On the outside, write "DO NOT OPEN UNTIL" and fill in a date—no fewer than 10 years from now.

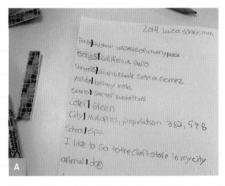

Seal your time capsule with duct tape.

5. Store your time capsule on a closet shelf, in the attic, or somewhere else it won't be disturbed. (Figure B) Or bury it out in the yard (with grownup supervision). If your family moves, don't forget to dig up the time capsule and bring it with you.

LEAF & FLOWER PRINTS

When you're exploring nature, it's fun to identify and collect different leaves and wildflowers.

Too often, though, your treasures end up getting tossed into the trash or compost. Before that happens, here's an easy way to artfully capture the essence of your leaves and flowers.

You'll need:

- Leaves and flowers, the more varied and colorful the better
- Paper (cardstock works well)
- Tape
- A hammer
- Cutting board or worktable

IMPORTANT! The US Forest Service discourages picking wildflowers in public forests and lands unless you have a permit and follow specific rules. Also, learn to recognize and avoid poison ivy, poison oak, and other plants that cause stings and rashes.

Try this:

1. Tape the corners of a piece of paper to the cutting board or worktable surface. If you don't have a worktable, place your cutting board onto a surface that won't get damaged—i.e., don't do this project on the dining room table or a nice wooden floor.

2. Arrange a few leaves and flowers (face up) on the paper in a way that looks good to you.

3. Place another piece of paper on top of your arrangement, and tape it in place.

4. Start hammering! Methodically pound every square inch of the paper with the hammer. Some color will seep into the top piece of paper while you're hammering; this is normal.

5. Gently separate the two pieces of paper, and scrape off any plant scraps. Choose whichever paper looks best, and tape it to the refrigerator. You're a nature artist!

SEW YOUR OWN
DITTY BAG

When sailors ship out to sea, they pack their "kit" (everything from toiletries to a pocket knife, to extra socks) into a handy drawstring sack known as a ditty bag.

Whether you're sailing, hiking, or heading out on a family road trip, a ditty bag is an essential piece of adventure gear. Here's how to sew your own.

You'll need:

- A piece of fabric that measures at least 22"x15". Nylon is a smart choice if you're packing liquid in containers that might leak. A fleece ditty bag can double as a pillow!
- A 46" length of nylon cord or paracord
- Measuring tape
- Pencil
- Scissors
- Sewing pins
- Safety pin
- Sewing machine with thread; or, if you're sewing by hand, a needle and thread.

Try this:

1. Using the tape measure, pencil, and scissors, mark, measure, and cut the fabric so that it measures 22"x15". Lay it flat on your work surface. The short sides will be vertical.

2. Sew a ¼" fold along the vertical sides of the fabric. While you're sewing, you'll probably want to use the sewing pins to hold the fold in place (Figure A); when you're done, remove the pins.

3. Now you'll create the "sleeve," through which you'll thread the ditty bag's drawstring. Lay the fabric out with the seams facing up; the short sides will be vertical. Fold the top 1" of the fabric over towards you. Pin it and sew, making sure that there is at least ½" between the edge of the fabric and your seam. (Figure B)

4. Fold the fabric in half so that the seams are facing out. It will now measure between 10" and 11" wide. Sew the bottom and side edge (one edge will be the folded fabric and won't need to be sewn), being careful to stop sewing just before you get to the bag's sleeve. (Figure C)

5. Turn the completed ditty bag right-side out (Figure D). Attach a safety pin to one end of the 46" length of cord, and thread the other end through the bag's sleeve. Remove the safety pin, and tie the cord's ends together with a square knot. (If you used paracord, with a grownup's supervision you can melt the two ends together using a lighter.)

6. Pack your adventure gear into the ditty bag, and head out!

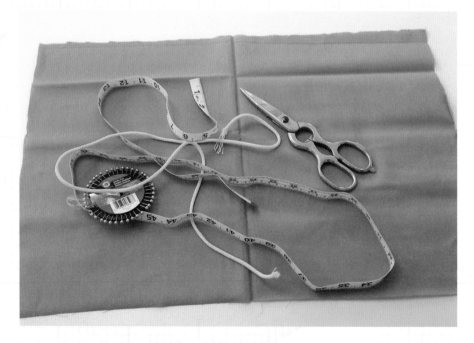

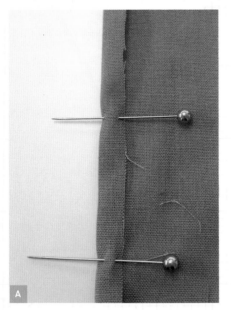

It's not just a survival tool, it's a fashion accessory.

When you're out in the wilderness, paracord can come in handy.

CRAFT A
PARACORD
BRACELET

Before you head out into the wild on an adventure, use a rainy day at home to make a paracord bracelet. Paracord was originally used in the suspension lines of US parachutes during World War II; once in the field, paratroopers found it useful for all sorts of things.

Not only does it look nifty, but this bracelet can be unraveled in an emergency—leaving you with 8' of lightweight nylon rope. Use it to secure a tarp, tie up a boat, even dry your clothes.

> **CAUTION!** When melting the ends of the bracelet, grownup supervision is a must.

Illustration by Heather Kasunick

You'll need:

- 4' each of nylon paracord (⅛" in diameter, also called "550 cord"), in two colors.
- A plastic side-release buckle (.60")
- Sharp scissors
- A lighter—use with grownup supervision
- Measuring tape
- Tape
- Pliers

Try this:

1. Measure the size of your wrist by wrapping the measuring tape snugly around it. Remember how many inches it is.

2. Using the scissors, cut two 4' pieces of paracord (one of each color, in this example yellow and gray).

3. With a grownup's help, and working in a well-ventilated space, use the lighter to melt the cut ends of each length of paracord—so the ends don't fray. Rotate each end in the flame for 3–4 seconds. While the melted ends are still hot, use the pliers to squeeze the ends flat.

4. Put both lengths of paracord together and thread them through the bottom slot of the "female" buckle piece. Make sure that when it is hanging below the cord, the buckle arcs inward.

5. At the opposite end of the combined paracords, thread them together through the bottom slot of the buckle's "male" piece. (This buckle should also arc inward.) Pull the cords about 1" or so through the slot, then fold this section over onto the rest of the paracord, and tape it there temporarily. (Figure A)

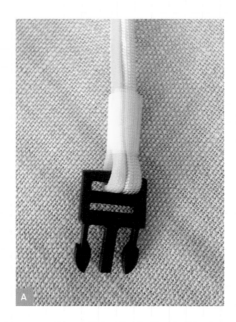

6. Remember your wrist measurement? Add 1" to that measurement (e.g., for a 6" wrist your total is 7"), then—using the measuring tape, and measuring from the slotted end of the male buckle instead of from its prongs—set the two buckles that distance (in this example, 7") apart from one another along the combined cords.

7. Lay the bracelet on a flat surface, with the female buckle at the top. The buckles will be arcing slightly upwards. This is the inside of the bracelet.

> **NOTE!** The photos on the following pages show a paracord bracelet whose first braid has already been knotted.

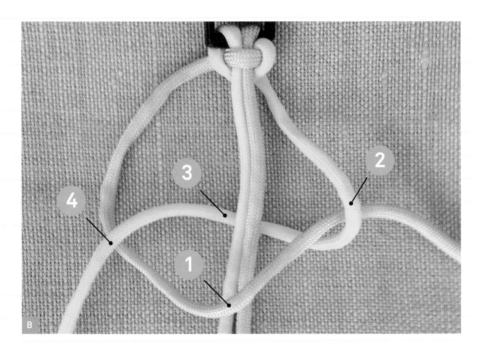

8. Hold the paracord you want to be the bracelet's inside color (in this example, gray) and make a loop to the left and then bring the end of the gray paracord to the right, over ① the two vertical paracords. Then take the second cord (in this example, yellow) and make a loop to the right. Thread the second cord (yellow) first over ② then under the gray cord and the two vertical paracords ③. Finally, thread the second (yellow) cord up through ④ the loop you created with the inside (gray) color cord. (Figure B) Tighten the braid and push it up toward the buckle. (Figure C)

9. Repeat Step 8 in reverse, by taking the inside color cord (gray) and making a loop to the right. Bring the end of the gray paracord to the left, under the two vertical paracords. Then take the second cord (in this example, yellow) and make a loop to the left. Thread the second cord (yellow) first under then over the gray cord—and then over the two vertical paracords. Finally, thread the second (yellow) cord up through the loop you created with the inside (gray) color cord.

10. Repeat Steps 8 and 9. (Figure D) When you get to the part of the cord where the excess cord is taped, while keeping the cord in place, remove the tape. Then repeat the weaving steps so that the formerly taped part is hidden underneath.

11. Braid right up to the edge of the buckle. Cut the cords so that no more than ¼" remains. Use the lighter to melt the ends into the bracelet. Press the cord into the bracelet with the pliers.

12. Show off your swag. (Figure E)

Humankind may have lived in trees thousands of years ago—for protection from scavenging animals, and because the light and climate are better up high.

In ancient Rome, the Emperor Caligula constructed a luxurious dining room—called the "Eyrie"—in the branches of a tree. Nobility in Persia had similar structures.

During the Middle Ages, Franciscan monks in Europe sometimes retreated to treehouses, where they'd meditate and work on their illuminated manuscripts.

A SECRET HISTORY

In the mid-16th century, Tuscany's powerful Medici family built elaborate treehouse retreats — complete with working fountains.

In the late 17th century, the Ottley family of England's Shropshire district constructed a treehouse at Pitchford Hall—which is still there. It's the world's oldest treehouse.

When Captain Cook—the first European explorer to circumnavigate New Zealand—visited Tasmania in the 1770s, he discovered native Tasmanians whose houses were built in trees.

Johann David Wyss's 1812 novel, THE SWISS FAMILY ROBINSON, about a shipwrecked Swiss family who builds a house in a tree, led to a modern-day European treehouse craze.

In 1848, a treehouse nightclub called "Le Grande Robinson" was built in the French village of Plessis. The town then became so popular that in 1909 it was renamed Le Plessis-Robinson.

Although characters — including Peter Pan, Tarzan, and Owl from WINNIE THE POOH — from several early 20th century fantasy novels live in treehouses, there was no new treehouse craze.

OF TREEHOUSES

In the middle of the 20th century, J.R.R. Tolkien's LORD OF THE RINGS described cool treehouses...and so did Jean Craighead George's MY SIDE OF THE MOUNTAIN. Still no craze.

In the late 1990s, environmental activist Julia "Butterfly" Hill illegally occupied a California Redwood tree for 738 days, in order to prevent a lumber company from cutting it down.

Since the early 2000s, elaborate recreational treehouses have enjoyed a rise in popularity — they've sprung up across the United States. Did "Butterfly" Hill spark a craze?

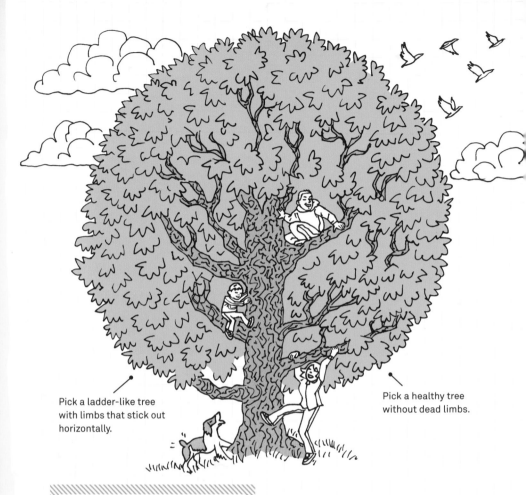

Pick a ladder-like tree with limbs that stick out horizontally.

Pick a healthy tree without dead limbs.

Illustration by Mister Reusch

CLIMB TREES

From the jungle gym to the geodesic dome to the climbing wall, humankind has designed many ingenious play structures. But none of these is so awe-inspiring as a tree.

Do your grownups worry about you falling out of a tree? Here are some tips to calm their fears about tree-climbing… and persuade them to give it a try, too.

Make a reasonable case

Grownups tend to find facts and figures reassuring. So tell yours that researchers in Norway and Sweden have determined that kids who are allowed to clamber up and around boulders, trees, and other natural play structures develop better balance and agility than do kids who hang out only in carefully regulated and monitored playgrounds.

You might also point out that plenty of accidents happen in playgrounds—in part because once you've jumped off the same monkey bars a few dozen times, you stop paying attention to what you're doing... which can lead to dangerous mistakes. When you're climbing a tree, you're in unfamiliar territory—so you tend to pay careful attention.

Learn to recognize good climbing trees

Tim Kovar, who founded a program called Tree Climbing Planet, strongly recommends that before you start climbing a tree you should inspect it carefully. You should look for a healthy tree without dead limbs; this is much easier to do in the late spring, summer, and early fall—when there are leaves or needles on the tree. You also want a ladder-like tree whose branches stick out horizontally, instead of aiming up or down.

Avoid trees with beehives, birds' nests, or squirrels' nests; their inhabitants are very protective of their turf. Avoid trees whose branches are growing around power lines. And don't climb during or immediately after a rainstorm—not only will the branches become slippery, but the tree might be struck by lightning.

Demonstrate proper technique

Show your grownup that you know what you're doing. Pick a tree whose lowest branches are close enough to the ground that you can easily climb onto and off the tree without assistance. Always place your feet and hands on the strongest part of the branch—closest to the tree's trunk. Remember to avoid branches that are dead or too small to support your weight.

When it's time to exit the tree, hang from the lowest branch and then drop gently to the ground. Absorb the impact by bending your knees. This advice is particularly important for your grownup—they need all the shock-absorption they can get.

Climb together

Encourage your grownup to climb a tree, too. If it's a large enough tree, you can climb together; otherwise, you can take turns. Don't rush them—let them take their time. Once your grownup climbs high enough into the tree, and sees the amazing view from up there, savor the moment together. It doesn't get much better than this sort of thing.

If your family wants to climb really big trees—including California's redwoods, even—check out a recreational tree-climbing school. These programs tend to use ropes and harnesses, to keep climbers safe; and, just as importantly, they use "branch savers" to protect the trees from harm. Some programs even let you sleep high up in a tree!

BICYCLING
MANIFESTO

By Eben Weiss

When the zombie apocalypse comes, what are you going to grab as you flee the flesh-eaters? Your plastic ninja sword? A bag of Doritos? A 24-pack of toilet paper?

I'm grabbing my bike. (OK, and the Doritos.) No machine heretofore invented is as practical as the bicycle. It requires no gasoline or electricity, and it's durable enough to travel mile after mile, day in and day out—yet it's light enough to carry up a flight of stairs.

A bike won't just save you from zombies. It will also save you from boredom. Here's how.

Get out of the house

I'm a blogger, so take it from me: If you sit inside all day, pawing at your electronics, you'll start to feel like your brain is being squeezed out of your ears. You've got to get out of the house.

If you have a bike, you don't need to beg someone for a ride, you don't need bus or train fare, and you don't need to consult a timetable. You can just *go*.

Make it an adventure

If you live someplace so remote that the most interesting thing within 100 miles is a Pizza Hut, then make the trip about the ride itself, not the destination.

Pick someplace far enough away that it will take you at least, say, a half hour to get there. The rhythm of turning the pedals gets your blood moving, and flushes any stagnant negativity out of your brain.

Illustrations by Mister Reusch

You'll begin to notice things that don't usually register: the wind in your face, the texture of the pavement, the topography of the neighborhood. When you fight your way up a hill, you'll be rewarded with the flight down the other side. Take a detour, hop a curb, explore a new street or alley. To paraphrase the slogan on Woody Guthrie's guitar: "This machine kills boredom."

Bond with your bike

The more often you ride, the more you'll learn about your machine. You'll make adjustments, maybe even attempt a repair. You'll add parts, modify them, or remove them, depending on how you like to ride. You'll make the bike your own.

Want to go faster? Change the tires, run higher air pressure, and get your shoulders down to cut through the wind. Want to go farther? Add a rack with saddlebags. The point here is that the bicycle can be a vehicle for self-expression. You can change the way it looks, the way it sounds, and the way it rides.

Keep exploring

There is no better key, when it comes to unlocking the mysteries of a town or city, than a bicycle. If you own a bike, you'll always have an alternative to transit delays, traffic, and (when you grow up) the burdens of car ownership. And you'll get to know your town inside out.

As the years go by, there's no telling where your bike will take you. You'll discover new places and meet new people. (On the other hand, sometimes the best thing about cycling is solitude.) From racing to touring to commuting, to just riding to the park or beach, there are whole worlds to be discovered on your bicycle.

A bike can be a vehicle for self-expression.

BIKE GEAR
TOP 10
By Eben Weiss

Helmet
It's good to have some protection on your noggin. Your helmet should sit level, right on top of your head—not tipped back like a beanie, not tipped forward like a fedora. The straps should be tight enough to keep the helmet in place, but not so tight that they hurt.

Lights
Unless you live in the Arctic Circle, the sun probably goes down at night where you live. When it does, you need lights. Even if you plan to be home before nightfall, sometimes you find yourself running late—and you're only as safe as you are visible.

Bag
There are all kinds of ways to carry stuff on your bike, from the coolest messenger bags to the most technical rack and pannier (saddlebag) systems, but you'll almost never go wrong with a good old-fashioned backpack.

Mini pump
A decent mini pump will fit in a pocket or bag yet give you enough air pressure to get you where you're going.

Food & water
One moment you feel like you can go forever, and the next you can barely turn over the pedals. So make sure you've got plenty to drink and lots of fast fuel: energy bars, granola, trail mix, Fig Newtons, cookies, bananas, chocolate bars... all of these are good for quickly stoking the furnace. Top off your water bottle at every opportunity.

Inner tubes & patch kit
No matter what you ride, where you ride, or how you ride, sooner or later you can count on getting a flat. Leave home prepared and you won't find yourself stranded. Practice flat repair at home first, so you won't have to learn on the side of the road.

Cash
Cycling's free, but that doesn't mean you should ride broke. You never know when you'll need some money when you're out having an adventure.

Multi-Tool
A multi-tool is a portable hand tool that combines several functions in a single unit; a bicycle multi-tool usually features the most common Allen key (or hex key) sizes. If something goes wrong, you'll be able to make adjustments or perform repairs.

Jacket
Unexpected cold and rain can ruin your ride, so if you're going to be out for a while, pack a jacket—or at least a hoodie.

Lock
The same things that make bicycles great—they're fast, they're lightweight—make them easy to steal. So don't leave your bike unattended without locking it.

PEDAL POWER!

Q&A with Elly Blue

A bicycle is much more than a vehicle for getting from one place to another, according to the Portland, Oregon–based publisher and activist Elly Blue. It's also a vehicle for social change!

In her books, including *Everyday Bicycling: How to Ride a Bike for Transportation* and *Bikenomics: How Bicycling Can Save the Economy*, as well as in zines and on her blog Taking the Lane, Blue demonstrates that bicycling is an adventure that can have a positive effect on our health, the environment, and on our community. We asked her for some advice.

Photo courtesy Caroline Paquette

UNBORED: What are the most important things you want people to know about bicycling?

BLUE: Because bikes don't pollute, biking is healthy for the planet. It's healthy for riders, too, thanks to all the exercise you get. And it's very practical—whether it's getting to school or a friend's house, or running errands, you can do anything that you need to do on a bike. But the most important thing to know about biking, I think, is that it's a great way to have a lot of fun.

UNBORED: Is there any essential bike gear that you recommend, for kids?

BLUE: Besides helmets, reflectors and lights are important—if you are going to ride your bicycle after dark. A bell is a very good way to let pedestrians and other bicyclists know that you are approaching from behind, not to mention a friendly way to say hello. If it's raining, fenders keep water and mud from splattering all over you. And a basket is handy—not only to carry the things you need, but so you can go on errands and help your family out.

UNBORED: You claim that in addition to being healthy for our bodies and the environment, biking is healthy for the social fabric of our communities. How so?

BLUE: You have probably noticed that when people are driving in cars, they are often unhappy and tend to get mad at other people—at pedestrians, other drivers, and bicyclists. But when you're riding a bike, you are usually happy and kinder to people. Biking gives us an easy way to meet each other face to face on the street, and to smile at each other, and do things together—and all of those things help you to get to know and like your neighbors.

A bicycle bell can be a friendly way to say hello.

UNBORED: How can kids use their bicycles to do something good for society?

BLUE: It's impossible to list all the amazing ways that you can use bikes to help others, but here are a few ideas off the top of my head. If you have a basket on your bike, you can deliver food to elderly shut-ins. If you're into picking up litter, then being on a bike allows you to cover a wider area than someone doing the same thing on foot. If you're concerned about the environment and keeping people healthy, you can organize a car-free day in your community—where you have a street party, and people learn new ways to get around.

UNBORED: Some grownups are worried about allowing their kids to explore on bicycles. Any safety tips? And any advice on how to persuade a grownup that biking is safe and healthy?

BLUE: If there's a class in your community that teaches bike safety skills, volunteer to take one so you can learn to signal your turns and ride confidently. Always look both ways, and assume that cars are going faster than they really are—and assume that they don't see you. Ask grownups who drive in your community to look out for bikes. Invite your grownup to go on rides with you, so they'll be comfortable with the route you're taking… and learn how fun it is.

Take a Biking Schoolbus to school in the morning.

UNBORED: Should kids bike to school in the morning?

BLUE: Yes! In addition to not using gas, biking to school helps kids focus in class—since they've gotten exercise and fresh air before school even starts. If you like the sound of biking to school, then you should persuade your school to have a bike-to-school day, and hopefully people will enjoy it so much they'll keep doing it. One really cool idea I've seen in action is the Biking Schoolbus, which is when a group of kids bikes to school together—usually accompanied by one or two grownups. Just like a schoolbus, the group picks each kid up at their "bus stop," so as you get closer to school the group grows larger and larger.

UNBORED: Biking on the sidewalk. Yes or no?

BLUE: Sometimes the sidewalk is a safer place to ride than the street—but in many ways, sidewalks are more dangerous. For example, when you're biking on the sidewalk, cars pulling in or out of driveways and alleys often can't see you. And intersections are dangerous when you're riding on the sidewalk, because drivers are only watching the street for traffic. The same thing is true of parking lots—drivers aren't looking out for bikers there. It's important that when you're not riding on the street, you stop and look at every opportunity. Also, pedestrians have the right of way on sidewalks, so you have to ride slowly and give them a lot of space. If there are a lot of people on the sidewalk, then get off your bike and walk instead.

Secret History OF Bicycles

1817

After crop failure causes the starvation of Germany's horses, Baron Karl von Drais invents a wooden riding machine without pedals. It's later nicknamed the "hobby-horse."

1885

English inventor John Kemp Starley produces a rear-wheel-drive, chain-driven riding machine with two similar-sized wheels. Starley's "safety bicycle" is the first modern bicycle.

1888

inflatable tires!

Scottish veterinarian John Dunlop applies pneumatic (inflatable) tires to his son's tricycle... an innovation that leads to bicycling finally becoming more comfortable and safe.

1934

Schwinn produces the "cruiser" bicycle. The bike's frame looks like a motorcycle (including a faux gas tank!) and sports "balloon" tires and a headlight.

1963

banana seat!

The bicycle manufacturer Huffy produces a children's bicycle whose design—"banana" seat and "ape hanger" handlebars-pays tribute to customized "chopper" motorcycles.

A French metalworker attaches pedals to the front wheel of a riding machine. Though bone-rattling, the "velocipede" (Latin for "fast foot") becomes the first popular riding machine.

A French inventor discovers that a large front wheel enables you to travel farther with each rotation of the pedals. This high-wheel machine is the first to be called a "bicycle."

During bicycling's Golden Age, women abandoned corsets and other restrictive clothing that had made cycling difficult. Susan B. Anthony calls the bicycle a "freedom machine."

French inventors make multi-speed bicycles possible thanks to systems consisting of a chain, multiple sprockets of different sizes, and a derailleur (chain-moving mechanism).

Stronger, heavier BMX bikes are invented because kids are so inspired by motocross racing that they're wrecking their standard bicycles by racing them on dirt tracks.

The first mountain bike, whose heavier frame and wider, knobbier tires are intended for off-road cycling, is mass-produced. The mountain biking craze begins...and it's still going.

AFTER-DARK
GAMES

Whether out in the street, at a nearby park, or in your own backyard, running around outdoors after dark is a fun adventure.

Are your grownups concerned about safety? Remind them that they used to play these games, too. Maybe you could even invite them to join in the fun.

Illustrations by Mister Reusch

KICK THE CAN

Adventurers: 5+

You'll need:

- An empty can (it's helpful to have a spare can handy)

Try this:

1. Agree on the boundaries of the game's playing area, and designate a "jail" space somewhere within this area. Designate one player as "It." (If you have over 10 players, then designate two players as "It.")

2. Just as the light is starting to fade, place a can in the middle of your playing area. The player who is "It" closes her eyes and counts aloud to 50. Everyone else scatters and hides. Note that you're allowed to switch hiding places during the game, if you want.

3. If you're "It," begin searching for hidden players. Whenever you spot someone, yell their name and try to tag them. If you succeed in tagging them, they are sent to jail. Players in jail can't speak— but they can signal to hiding players with their hands.

4. However, if the person who was spotted eludes "It" and kicks the can, then all players who were in jail are freed. It's customary to shout, "Kick the can, everyone's free!" Note that hiding players don't have to wait to be spotted before they try to kick the can.

5. Whenever the can is kicked, "It" must close her eyes and count to 50 aloud while the freed players scatter and hide.

6. Once "It" has captured all players, the game ends.

SAFETY FIRST

Ground rules

Sometimes you might be so well hidden that the game ends and you don't even realize it. So if you hear people calling "All in free," or shouting your name, it's not funny to keep hiding.

Plan ahead

If you're playing in an unfamiliar place, everyone should be carrying a flashlight— even if they're not allowed to use it during the game. At least one player should be carrying a phone, in case of an emergency. And make sure to establish a meeting place, preferably one that is illuminated by a streetlight, in case someone gets lost.

Watch your step

Although you want good places to hide, beware of obstacles that you might run into in the dark: fire hydrants, park benches, boulders, and so forth. Be particularly careful of moving vehicles.

FIREFLY

Adventurers: 3+

You'll need:

• A flashlight (several, if you are playing with a large group)

Try this:

1. If you have 10 or fewer people, designate one player to be the "firefly." If you have over 10 people, designate two or more fireflies. Issue a flashlight to each firefly.

2. If you're a firefly, run and hide—while counting silently to 60. At the same time, the others players (the seekers) close their eyes and count aloud to 30.

3. Once the seekers count to 30, they spread out in search of the firefly or fireflies.

4. Once the fireflies count to 60, they must switch their flashlights on and off quickly... creating a flickering effect. Just for a moment, though.

5. Once the flickering stops, the seekers count aloud to 20, then rush towards where they saw the flashlight or flashlights flickering. Meanwhile, the fireflies sneak away under cover of darkness... while counting silently to 60 again.

6. Repeat Steps 3 and 4 until the firefly or fireflies are captured.

WEEPING ANGELS TAG

Adventurers: 10+

On the British sci-fi show *Dr. Who,*
Weeping Angels are predators who
resemble statues.

You'll need:

- 3 flashlights
- Very dark playing field or large empty
  room with the lights turned off
- A timer or stopwatch; use one on your
  phone, if you have one

Try this:

1. Designate one player as Dr. Who, and
    two players as Dr. Who's companions.
    Issue a flashlight to each of these
    three players. The other players are
    Weeping Angels; one of them must set
    a timer or stopwatch that will beep
    15 minutes after the start of play.

2. Start the clock! The Weeping Angels
    close their eyes and count—in creepy
    voices—aloud to 25. Meanwhile,
    Dr. Who and his two companions
    scatter and hide.

3. Once the Weeping Angels have counted
    to 25, they spread out and search for
    the hiding players. The rule is that they
    can only move when they're not being
    watched. So if you're a Weeping Angel,
    and Dr. Who or one of the companions
    shines a flashlight on you, freeze in
    place. If you're Dr. Who or one of the
    companions, don't shine the light for
    very long, because doing so will attract
    Weeping Angels towards you.

4. If you're Dr. Who or one of the com-
    panions and you're tagged, die with a
    dramatic groan. The game ends when
    all three of you are dead, or once
    15 minutes have passed.

Remain in a state of constant vigilance!

ASSASSIN GAME

Adventurers: 5+, the more the merrier

A "pervasive" game is one that surrounds you even as you go about your normal routine, transforming everyday life into an adventure.

Assassin (aka Killer, Gotcha, Paranoia; Nerf War is an informal version) was invented on college campuses in the 1960s. You are assigned to "kill" another player with a toy weapon… while avoiding the player who has been assigned to "kill" you. You can stalk or be stalked any time, anywhere, so you must remain in a state of constant vigilance. The game might last for weeks, but we prefer the following version, which can be played during a weekend gathering.

Illustration by Mister Reusch

You'll need:

- A non-playing game moderator
- Squirt guns, magic markers

Try this:

1. The moderator announces to all players when the game will begin—say, at 8 pm on Friday.

2. Before the start of the game, the moderator will assign you a target. This assignment might take the form of a name scribbled on a piece of paper, or perhaps a photo sent to your phone. Always keep your target a secret from other players! At the same time, the moderator will deliver your name or photo to another player; you're now *their* target. Note that the moderator should never assign two players to stalk each other.

3. You must stalk and attempt to "assassinate" your target—by shooting them with a squirt gun, or marking their skin with a marker. Note that the moderator will usually specify rules, such as:

- No hand-to-hand combat; no stabbing someone with the marker.

- You must be alone when you assassinate your target; no eye-witnesses!

- Certain areas are designated as "safe zones."

- Disputes between two players are ruled on by the moderator.

- If you "kill" your target, then that player is out of the game. They must pass along information about their own target to you; your new assignment is to stalk and "kill" that player. Before you do so, you should report your "kill" to the game moderator and reveal who your new target is.

- When there are only two people left in the game, they're declared the winners.

BEST EVER

URBAN EXPLORATION APPS

Taking a selfie at your local pizzeria? Meh. Using an ingenious app that harnesses the collective intelligence of its users—including you!—to discover the best pizza in town? Now we're talking.

Our favorite smartphone apps offer you boredom-busting opportunities to get out of your usual routine and explore unknown territory… which might be closer to home than you'd expected.

IMPORTANT! Users of these apps must be 13 to subscribe, and the online interaction isn't moderated. So kids under 13 can and should only use these apps with their grownups.

Atlas Obscura

Atlasobscura.com

Not an app but a website, Atlas Obscura aims to be the definitive guide to the world's strangest and most amazing destinations, including: an abandoned particle collider in Texas; the Louisville, Kentucky, grave of Colonel Sanders; New York's Graffiti Hall of Fame; the lowest point in North America (in Death Valley, California); the world's first zoo for microbes; and a statue in Elberton, Georgia, that was torn down by an angry mob because it looked stupid.

On page 28 of this book you'll find a Q&A with the founders of Atlas Obscura.

Foodspotting

Foodspotting.com

Craving fish tacos? Sushi? Eclairs? Search for dumplings, French toast, nachos, frozen yogurt, or whatever it is you love eating, and Foodspotting will present you with photos—uploaded by your fellow food lovers, shortly before they chowed down—and brief reviews of the best options around. Unlike similar apps for foodies, this one doesn't publish negative reviews… so instead of wasting your time weighing pros and cons and reading trash-talk, you can head out for a snack.

Foursquare

Foursquare.com

This app is a game that learns what you like, leads you to places you will most likely enjoy, and rewards you—with digital merit badges, like "Adventurer," "Explorer," "Greasy Spoon," "Trainspotter," and "I'm On a Boat"—for going somewhere and trying something new. Whenever you check in to a location, Foursquare (or rather, its 50 million users) will recommend cool places to go and fun things to do nearby.

Illustrations by Heather Kasunick

Google Maps
Google.com/maps
Whether you need directions to travel by foot, car, bus, or bicycle, Google Maps, the mother of all exploration apps, helps you get wherever you want to go. Among its many amazing functions, you can view live traffic, take the most scenic route to your destination, plan a route with multiple destinations (great for a family road trip), locate places of interest (en.touristpath.com), and create your own custom maps. To do the latter, drop pins into your favorite spots using the My Maps feature—and then invite family and friends to suggest new places to visit.

Historypin
Historypin.org
This app asks users worldwide to upload family photos—your grandfather in Ho Chi Mihn City during the Vietnam War, say, or your mother's school photos—and "pin" them to a particular location using Google Maps. When you're walking around your own neighborhood or town, it's fun to use Historypin to see how things have changed over the years. Cobblestone streets? Horse-drawn trolleys? An ice cream parlor where the mobile phone store is now?

Who knew? You can also use the app to travel around the world, without leaving home.

Oh Ranger!
Ohranger.com
Whether you want to find a skate park or hiking trail, this comprehensive database of every federal and state park in America (not to mention neighborhood parks) is an awesome tool. On vacation, or just looking for a good excuse to get outside and explore? Search the Oh, Ranger! website or the Oh, Ranger! ParkFinder app by zipcode or activity—bicycling, camping, climbing, fishing, horseback riding, picnicking, you name it—and you'll be directed to nearby parks, along with photos and reviews from fellow outdoor enthusiasts.

Trover
Trover.com
Visually oriented? Trover detects your location, then guides you to things nearby that you might like to check out, by showing you dozens of geo-tagged photos uploaded by fellow users; think of it as Instagram for explorers. The first photos you'll see are nearby locations, and the more you scroll down, the farther you'll have to travel in order to get to the locations pictured. Trover also features helpful lists that you can use to search for particular kinds of attractions.

BUILD AN ADVENTURE

LAUNCH AN
UPCYCLED
RAFT

Recycling has never been more fun.

A little scavenging should turn up all the empty milk or juice cartons and jugs you'll need to build an upcycled raft.

Perhaps you think of sailboats, canoes, and kayaks as the best ways to travel over water? Mark Twain's character Huckleberry Finn might disagree… and so would real-life explorer Thor Heyerdahl, who in 1947 sailed across the Pacific on a raft he named *Kon-Tiki*.

While we don't recommend taking your homemade raft down a river (currents can be dangerous), you can build it in a single morning and spend the rest of the day paddling it around your favorite lake or pond.

You'll need:

- 24 1-gallon milk or water jugs, rinsed and empty—with the caps screwed on, or (if they don't have caps) the openings sealed with hot glue
- 24 2-quart milk or juice cartons—same instructions as above. **Optional:** Instead of 24 1-gallon jugs plus 24 2-quart cartons, you can use 36 1-gallon jugs.
- Glue gun and lots of glue refills; use with grownup supervision.
- A 42"x60" sheet of ⅜" plywood. You can have them cut it to size at the lumberyard, or else have your grownup cut it with a saw. Make sure she wears safety goggles!
- A 60-yard roll of industrial strength 2" duct tape
- A kayak paddle
- A personal flotation device (PFD)
- **Optional:** Collapsible trail chair

Illustrations by Mister Reusch

Try this:

1. Scavenge all the jugs and/or cartons you'll need. You can trash-pick them from recycling bins, and ask your neighbors and friends to save jugs and cartons for you. (It might take weeks or months to gather enough jugs and cartons, so start doing so right away!) (Figure A) Rinse out your jugs and cartons, so they don't stink—then screw the caps on tightly, or cover the openings with duct tape and use the hot glue gun to seal the openings closed. Use the glue on the capped containers, too, to create a seal between the cap and the bottle. (Figure B)

2. While you're gathering supplies, design your raft—based on weight requirements. A 1-gallon jug can float approximately 8 lbs., and a 2-quart carton can float approximately 4 lbs., so the (24 1-gallon jugs, 24 2-quart cartons) raft we're describing here ought to float over 250 lbs. Our test model takes on a bit of water at 175 lbs., but doesn't sink even at 250! Remember to factor in the weight of the plywood.

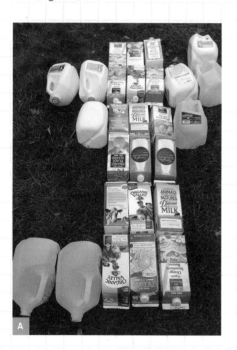

> **IMPORTANT!** Make sure you have grownup supervision when you use a glue gun. Wear long pants so that you don't accidentally get burned. Tighten the nozzle before you plug it in and remember to unplug the glue gun after you are finished.

3. Working in a well-ventilated space—preferably in the open air—lay the plywood down flat on a worktable or sawhorses, because you'll want to reach underneath.

4. Arrange your jugs and/or cartons onto the plywood, in such a way as to provide maximum stability when the raft is afloat. We decided to make two "pontoons," one on each side of the raft; each pontoon was a 2x6 row of 1-gallon jugs. We filled in the space between the pontoons with six rows of containers—each row can either consist of 4 2-quart cartons, or 2 1-gallon jugs. The jugs are more buoyant, but the cartons will work.

5. Once you've figured out where all the jugs and/or cartons will fit, plug in the hot glue gun and start gluing the jugs and/or cartons into place—using just a dollop of glue each time. Start by gluing down the pontoons, then fill in the interior rows of jugs or cartons. (Figure C)

6. Now tape the jugs and/or cartons down, with the duct tape. Using long lengths of duct tape, secure each row both horizontally and vertically, securing the two ends of each length of tape onto the reverse side of the plywood. (Figure D) You'll want someone to help you do this part, because as one person stretches the tape the other should smooth it down tightly—making sure that it adheres to all of the jugs and cartons. When you're finished, the entire underside of the raft should be more or less covered with duct tape.

7. Flip the raft over. Using more long lengths of duct tape, cover all the tape ends around the raft's edges. Do this along all four sides, and lay down two layers of tape for extra security. This will also make the edges of your raft look tidy and well-framed. (Figure E)

8. Put on your PFD, tote your raft to a body of water, and—with grownup supervision—use the kayak paddle to navigate your new adventure vehicle. We found that sitting in a collapsible trail chair while you paddle is both more comfortable and more efficient. (Figure F)

Use a dollop of hot glue to hold each jug or carton in place.

HOW TO SURVIVE
SUSTAINABLY

AN EXCERPT FROM

THE SWISS FAMILY ROBINSON

by Johann David Wyss

In *The Swiss Family Robinson* (1812), when a Swiss pastor, his wife, their four sons (Fritz, Ernest, Jack, and Franz), and two dogs (Turk and Flora) are shipwrecked in the East Indies, they don't despair. The resilient group figures out how to produce everything they need from soap to rain boots, build an amazing treehouse, and feed themselves—without ever ruining the fragile ecosystem of their new home.

We proceeded towards a pleasant wood of palm-trees; but before reaching it, had to pass through an immense number of reeds, which greatly obstructed our road. We were, moreover, fearful of treading on the deadly serpents who choose such retreats. We made Turk walk before us to give notice, and I cut a long, thick cane as a weapon of defence. I was surprised to see a glutinous juice oozing from the end of the cut cane; I tasted it, and was convinced that we had met with a plantation of sugar-canes. I sucked more of it, and found myself singularly refreshed. I said nothing to Fritz, that he might have the pleasure of making the discovery himself. He was walking a few paces before me, and I called to him to cut himself a cane like mine, which he did, and soon found out the riches it contained.

He cried out in ecstasy, 'Oh, papa! papa! syrup of sugar-cane! delicious! How delighted will dear mamma, and my brothers be, when I carry some to them!' He went on, sucking pieces of cane so greedily, that I checked him, recommending moderation. He was then content to take some pieces to regale himself as he walked home, loading himself with a huge burden for his mother and brothers.

We now entered the wood of palms to eat our dinner, when suddenly a number of monkeys, alarmed by our approach, and the barking of the dog, fled like lightning to the tops of the trees; and then grinned frightfully at us, with loud cries of defiance. As I saw the trees were cocoa-palms, I hoped to obtain, by means of the monkeys, a supply of the nuts in the half-ripe state, when filled with milk. I held Fritz's arm, who was preparing to shoot at them, to his great vexation, as he was irritated against the poor monkeys for their derisive gestures; but I told him, that though no patron of monkeys myself, I could not allow it. We had no right to kill any animal except in defence, or as a means of supporting life. Besides, the monkeys would be of more use to us living than dead, as I would show him. I began to throw stones at the monkeys, not being able, of course, to reach the place of their retreat, and they, in their anger, and in the spirit of imitation, gathered the nuts and hurled them on us in such quantities, that we had some difficulty in escaping from them. We had soon a large stock of cocoa-nuts.

Fritz enjoyed the success of the stratagem, and, when the shower subsided, he collected as many as he wished. We then sat down, and tasted some of the milk through the three small holes, which we opened with our knives. We then divided some with our hatchets, and quenched our thirst with the liquor, which has not, however, a very agreeable flavour. We liked best a sort of thick cream which adheres to the shells, from which we scraped it with our spoons, and mixing it with the juice of the sugar-cane, we produced a delicious dish. Turk had the rest of the lobster, which we now despised, with some biscuit.

We then got up, I tied some nuts together by their stems, and threw them over my shoulder. Fritz took his bundle of canes, and we set out homewards.

TRASH NIGHT
TREASURE HUNT

By Tony Leone

The evening before the garbage truck comes around is the perfect time to prowl your neighborhood—or perhaps a fancier neighborhood than yours—in search of awesome stuff.

Your mission: Bring home something amazing that you found on the curb. Hurry! Before someone else beats you to it.

Bikes

People often throw out perfectly good bicycles—usually because they've been outgrown. So keep an eye peeled for quality bike brands like Haro, Trek, or GT. Flat tires, missing hand brakes, torn seats, and other minor problems can be fixed at a bike shop for a modest fee. But if the frame is broken, bent, or completely rusted, then leave the bicycle where it is.

Toys

Cloth dolls and their outfits can get moldy, dusty, and gross (so don't trash-pick Beanie Babies). Old battery-powered toys are often useless, because their batteries have corroded. But if they're not broken, then toys made from wood, metal, and plastic ought to be OK. We recently found a Fisher Price "Play Family" Airport set from 1972 in perfect condition. Score!

Books

Why do people throw away books? That's crazy—they should donate them to a library sale. Oh well, their mistake is your opportunity to discover vintage editions of your favorite books (a complete set of the Encyclopedia Brown books, in hardcover, say), not to mention terrific old kids' books (like Holling C. Holling's *Paddle-to-the-Sea*) of which you've never even heard!

Smelly stuff

No matter how cool an object looks, if it smells moldy you don't want it. Mold can cause allergic reactions and respiratory problems—and besides, it's just plain gross. Some mold doesn't smell, so watch out for discoloration and little dark speckles, particularly on books.

Fun oddities

Trash-picking isn't just about finding things you need. It's about the joy of exploration and discovery; it's like going to an open-air museum where you can bring home the artworks. Look for things that your family would never purchase in a million years: fluorescent orange desk lamps, mannequin heads, Elvis records, mermaid-shaped bottles. If it appeals to you, snag it!

CAUTION! Never look for curbside treasures in trash cans.

BUILD AN ADVENTURE

THROW SEED GRENADES

Seed grenades were first used centuries ago. By packing seeds into a just-sturdy-enough vessel, which might also contain some fertilizer, farmers ensured that their precious seeds were protected from birds, insects, sun, and wind until rainfall caused them to germinate. Ingenious!

In the 1970s, seed balls were rediscovered and popularized by Japanese "Do-Nothing Farming" pioneer Masanobu Fukuoka. Around the same time, guerrilla gardening pioneer Liz Christy began throwing wildflower "seed grenades" into fenced-off vacant lots around her New York neighborhood.

You'll need:

- Seeds of three distinct species of wildflowers native to your area
- 1 lb. or so of organic compost
- Air-dry clay (for example, the kind sold by Crayola)
- Newspaper torn into 2"-wide strips
- 2½ cups of flour
- One dozen eggs
- Mixing bowls
- Towels you can get dirty
- Water
- Small balloons
- A long nail
- A small straw
- Masking tape

Illustration by Mister Reusch

118 | URBAN ADVENTURE
| Throw Seed Grenades

Clay Seed Grenades

1. Mix a small amount of clay with compost and just enough water to form a mix that holds together without crumbling.

2. Pinch off a small amount of the mixture, stick a few of the first variety of wildflower seeds into it, and roll it into a ball. Roll the ball in more compost.

3. Make a dozen or so of these clay seed grenades, then leave them to dry on a windowsill or counter.

Papier-mâché Seed Grenades

1. Blow up a dozen or so balloons—until they're no bigger than your fist.

2. Mix the flour with 3 cups of water, until it has a pancake batter consistency.

3. Dip the newspaper into the mixture, then squeegee off the excess gunk with your fingers.

4. Wrap each inflated balloon with papier-mâché (that's what you've made), leaving an empty space about as big as a coin around the balloon's knot. Once the shells have dried, pop and remove the balloons.

5. Fill each shell with compost mixed with a tiny bit of water, and a few of the second variety of seeds. Put a piece of tape over the papier-mâché seed grenade's hole.

Eggshell Seed Grenades

1. Using the nail, poke a small hole at the center of the egg's smaller end, and a larger hole at the other end; then use the nail to break the yolk.

2. Using the straw, blow the contents of the egg out of the larger hole into a bowl. Because you're not using these eggshells for a craft, you don't need to clean them out perfectly.

3. Tape the small hole closed, then fill the eggshell with compost, a little water, and a few of the third variety of seeds. Put a piece of tape over the eggshell seed grenade's hole.

Ready to make like Johnny Appleseed?

With grownup supervision, toss the seed grenades into untended public spots. The idea is that they'll break on impact.

Keep visiting these spots and take notes—which species of flower grows best?

ROAM!

When you're exploring the neighbor-hood, or going farther afield, does your grownup skulk along a few steps behind you?

It's nice of them to make sure you're safe! However, if you start small and build up to bigger adventures, then soon enough you'll be allowed to strike out on your own. Here are some ways to get started.

Explore downtown

There's a whole world out there beyond the end of your block. Take the bus or train downtown, or to the next town over, and check out a skate park, museum, or shoe store. The key to success in your explo-ration is planning. Before you head out, discuss your plans for the trip with your grownup; ask them to look at a map with you and identify areas you should avoid. Bring enough money for your bus or train fare, plus money for a snack. Start heading home well before it gets dark outside.

Grab a bite

Going out with friends for a meal is a great way to demonstrate your inde-pendence. Ask your grownup for a little "walking-around money," then walk or bike to an eatery in your area. It's OK if your grownup wants to tag along the first time—but they can only do so once! As long as they're along for the ride, ask your grownup to demonstrate bussing (cleaning up) and tipping.

Illustration by Mister Reusch

Catch a bus or train

Getting around town without asking your grownup for a ride can be liberating for both of you! But nothing makes grownups more nervous than the thought of you getting lost. So soothe their fears by taking a few trial runs on the bus or subway together. Once you know the route (including landmarks to watch out for, how to signal for the bus to stop, and so forth), it's time to go solo. Make sure you have enough money for a round-trip fare. And stay alert! You'll feel silly if you miss your stop because you were fiddling with your phone.

Take a spin

Encourage your grownup to take bike rides around the neighborhood with you—but have them ride behind you! This way, you can demonstrate that you know how to signal turns, come to a full stop at stop signs, walk your bike through inter-sections, and know the best routes from your home to the pizza place, a friend's house, or wherever you like to go. Next, persuade your grownup to let you make these trips on your own.

Get to know your local bus route.

PHONE
HOME

If you have a phone, bring it on your adventures—there are great apps you can use to explore your city and check bus and subway schedules. If you are new to heading out on your own, you can also use it to reassure your grownups that everything is going fine. We suggest calling or texting your grownups twice: when you arrive at your destination and then when you are on your way home. Save telling them what kind of ice cream you ordered for when you see them in person. Once you get the hang of exploring without your grownups, you can stick to one call or text to let them know when to expect you back.

SHOOTIN' CRAPS

Adventurers: 2+, the more the merrier

Craps is a dice game played crouching down, like a toad. In fact, the game's name is derived from *crapaud*, the French word for toad.

Why is craps played crouching, instead of sitting? Because traditionally, it was a gambling game—so you had to be ready to jump to your feet and run from the police at any minute.

You'll need:
• A pair of six-sided dice

Try this:

1. Gather in an alley near a fence, wall, or curb—this will be your game's backstop.

2. On your turn, shoot the dice—that is to say, roll them vigorously along the ground at the fence, wall, or curb; the dice should hit your backstop and bounce back. Why? Because that way, everybody knows you didn't cheat.

3. If you shoot a 7 or 11 on your "come-out" (first) roll, then you immediately win! But if you shoot a 7 or 11 on any roll *after* your come-out roll, you lose.

4. If you shoot a 2, 3, or 12 on your come-out roll, then you immediately lose. However, it's OK to shoot a 2, 3, or 12 on any roll after your come-out roll.

5. If you shoot a "point" number (4, 5, 6, 8, 9, or 10), then you keep shooting the dice until you either match the point number (that is, by rolling the same number again) or you roll a 7 or 11.

6. Did you match your point number? You win! If you rolled a 7 or 11, you lose.

CRAPS ROLLS

2: Snake Eyes or Aces
3: Ace Deuce
4: Ballerina (2-2, get it?) or Little Joe (1-3)
5: Fever Five or Little Phoebe
6: Jimmie Hicks
7: Natural (on the come-out roll), otherwise Seven Out
8: Square Pair or Ozzie and Harriet (4-4), otherwise Eighter from Decatur
9: Jesse James (4-5), otherwise Niner from Carolina
10: Puppy Paws (5-5), otherwise Best Friend
11: Six-Five, No Jive (on the come-out roll), otherwise Yo-leven
12: Boxcars

Illustration by Heather Kasunick

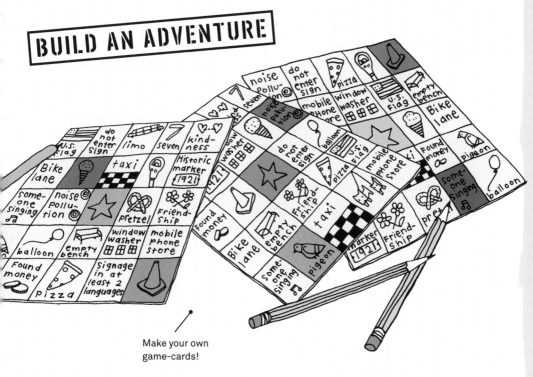

Make your own game-cards!

URBAN
BINGO

Adventurers: 3 to 7

Sometimes, the only thing standing between you and an adventure in and around your own town is a good excuse to go exploring. So here's the perfect excuse.

Bingo, a game of chance played on a grid of 25 squares, was first popularized in America in the 1930s. By the '50s, families on road trips were playing a version called *Auto Bingo*—in which the game-card's squares were filled with targets that you might spot during the drive, like a billboard or truck. Urban Bingo applies the same notion to cities.

You'll need:

- 24 targets. The idea is to challenge players to travel around town together, in search of a hot dog cart, say, or a taxicab, a pigeon, a mobile phone store, or a construction site.
- Game-cards.
- Pens or pencils, for marking off targets once they're spotted.

Illustrations by Heather Kasunick

Make the game-cards

1. On pieces of paper or cardboard, draw 5x5 grids of squares

2. Fill each of the 25 spaces *except* the center square (a "free space") with your 24 targets. Arrange the 24 targets in a different order for each game-card.

3. If you think you'll want to reuse the same game-cards in the future, then you should make photocopies.

Play the game

1. Everyone can get started by marking off the "free space" at their card's center.

2. Although each player has her own unique game-card, and is competing against the others in the group, the group *must stick together at all times*. It's a group adventure.

3. If a player spots one of the game-card's 24 targets (a taxicab, say), she must announce it—"Taxicab!"—loudly. But before she can mark this target off her game-card, the other members of the group must corroborate that what she saw was, indeed, what she claimed. Nobody else is allowed to spot the same target; find your own taxicab.

If you're the first to spot one of the game's targets, shout it out.

4. If you're the first member of your group to mark off five squares in a vertical, diagonal, or horizontal line across your game-card, then you win. Whoever is the first to fill up their entire game-card is the runner-up; it might be the same winner in both cases.

➡ **HACKS** - - - - - - - - -

- In addition to a straight line, dozens of other patterns of marked-off squares may be considered as valid bingos. (See "Bingo Lingo" for a few examples.)
- Allow representations of targets to count. If one of your game's targets is "taxicab," and you spot someone wearing a t-shirt with a drawing of a taxicab on it, then it counts!
- In addition to people, places, and things, use abstract concepts—like "noise pollution," "security," "waste," "friendship"—for a few of your game's 24 targets. This hack is guaranteed to make corroboration discussions among your group more lively.

BINGO LINGO

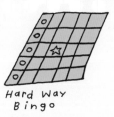

Hard Way Bingo

Hard Way Bingo
A bingo pattern in a straight line without the use of the free space.

"I have a chance"
This means you only need to mark off one final square in order to complete a bingo. You'd say this in order to alert your fellow players that you're about to win the game. You might also say, "I'm cased," "I'm on," or "I'm down."

Bongo
Calling "bingo" before you have a valid bingo. How embarrassing.

Blackout
A winning pattern in which *all* squares of the game-card are marked off. As with the following game types, this is something that would be announced in advance.

Postage Stamp
A 2x2 square of marked-off spaces in the game-card's upper right corner. In order to win some Bingo games, players are required to mark off a "postage stamp" pattern; that is, they can't win until they've filled the four top-right squares.

Roving "L"
A winning pattern, in some games, in which all five squares in the card's left-hand column, plus all five squares on the bottom row (for example), are marked off.

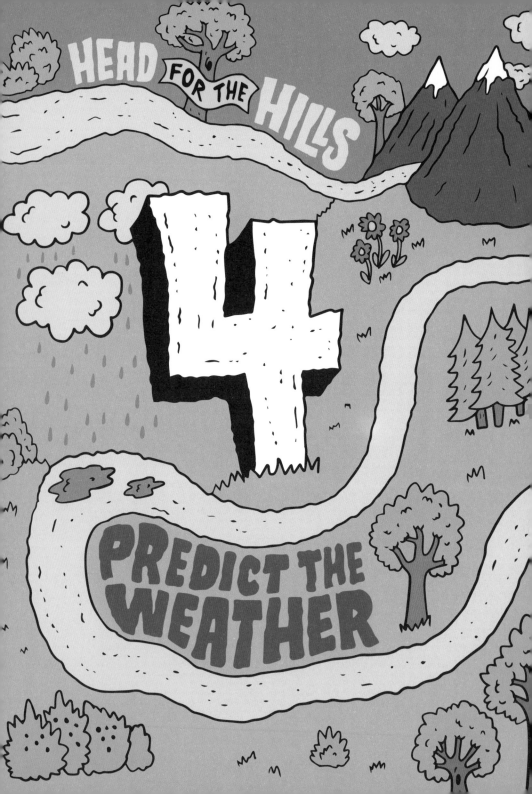

SURVIVAL
SCIENCE

By Liz Lee Heinecke

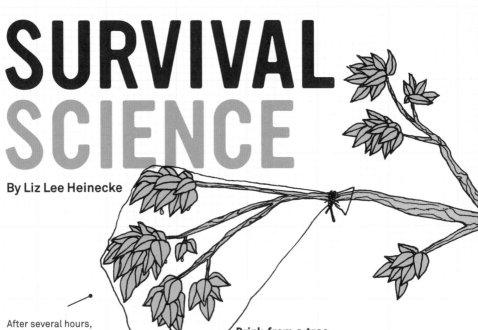

After several hours, condensation will collect inside the plastic bag.

When you step outside, you step into nature's laboratory.

Scientists study our fascinating planet by developing hypotheses (educated guesses) about how nature works. They test these hypotheses, then draw conclusions based on the results of these tests. Doing science goes hand-in-hand with adventures in nature.

Here are three survival-science projects that rely on the earth's very own star, the sun—an abundant, free energy source that you can take advantage of while exploring.

Drink from a tree

On a sunny day, you can collect drinkable water by utilizing a biological process called *transpiration*, where a plant's leaves release water from small pores (*stomata*) on their bottom side. All you need is a large, transparent plastic bag.

1. A leafy tree is ideal for water collection. Enclose the end of a branch and as many of its leaves as possible in the transparent plastic bag—adding a small, clean pebble in order to weigh one corner of the bag down.

2. Tie the bag tightly around the branch, so moisture can't escape.

3. After several hours, water molecules from the tree will have condensed and collected inside the bag.

   Since you used a transparent bag, the sun's ultraviolet radiation will have killed most of the harmful microbes.

Illustrations by Heather Kasunick

Warm up a snack

As we've just seen, a container sealed with clear plastic wrap can trap the sun's energy. You can use this same knowledge to turn a pizza box, aluminum foil, clear plastic wrap, black paper, and newspaper into a solar oven. You'll also need a cutting tool and tape.

1. With grownup supervision, cut a hinged flap into the top of the pizza box, leaving about 2" of the box's lid on each side.

2. Fold the flap back and cover its underside with aluminum foil; this shiny reflector will focus the sun's rays into your oven.

3. Stretch and tape a piece of clear plastic wrap over each side of the hole you've cut, creating a double-paned oven window.

4. Cover the bottom of the pizza box's inside with black paper—because a black surface efficiently absorbs the sun's radiation.

5. Tightly roll up sheets of newspaper and tape them around the inside perimeter of the bottom of your solar oven; the newspaper will prevent the sun's trapped heat from escaping.

6. On a sunny day, set a snack that needs warming up—perhaps something involving chocolate or cheese—on the black paper inside your solar oven.

7. Close the pizza box's lid, and prop open the reflective flap with a stick. Angle the solar oven so that the sun's rays are reflected off the aluminum foil and through the double-paned window.

When the chocolate or cheese begins to melt, open the lid of your oven and enjoy your snack!

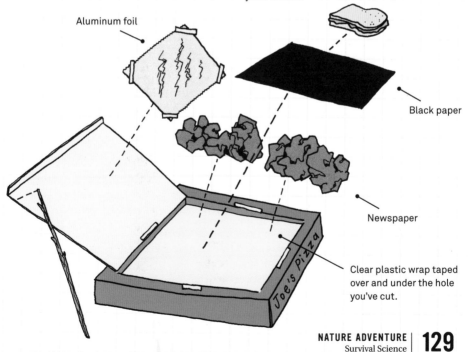

Aluminum foil

Black paper

Newspaper

Clear plastic wrap taped over and under the hole you've cut.

Purify water

You should always purify water collected from lakes or streams before you drink it, because invisible microbes are everywhere. One way to purify water is to build a solar still using two nested bowls and a sheet of plastic wrap.

1. Put a few inches of water into the larger of the two bowls, then place the smaller bowl into the larger one. Don't let the unpurified water spill into the smaller bowl!

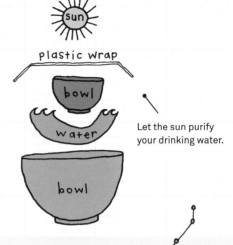

Let the sun purify your drinking water.

MY FAMILY'S
10 FAVORITE SCIENCE APPS
By Liz Lee Heinecke

Magnificent
habitualdigitalsoftware.com
Ready for a close up? This magnifying-glass app gives you a bug's-eye view of nature. Make sure to hold it steady for a clear view.

Starmap
star-map.fr
Whether you're sleeping under the stars or throwing an impromptu stargazing party, Starmap points you to the celestial bodies visible from your location.

ISS Spotter
Via the iTunes Store
This app lets you know when the International Space Station will be flying over your area and where to look for the speeding light blinking brighter than the stars. You can even set an alarm to remind you to run outside and look up!

Geocaching
geocaching.com/mobile/
This app elevates routine errands and hikes to adventure status, by leading you to hidden caches everywhere from suburban soccer fields to remote mountaintops. If you're headed to an area with no cellular service, save cache coordinates to your smartphone ahead of time.

Leafsnap
leafsnap.com
Can you tell a maple from an oak? This app lets you use the camera on your smartphone to shoot a picture of a leaf or pine needle and easily identify the tree it came from.

2. Cover the larger bowl's mouth with the plastic wrap, using a small stone to weigh the plastic down in the middle. The plastic wrap shouldn't touch the smaller bowl.

3. Place your solar water purifier in a sunny spot, and wait for a few hours.

4. Heated water molecules will evaporate into the air and condense in droplets on the underside of the plastic wrap—which is cooler than the heated water, because it's exposed to the outside air.

Condensation from the underside of the plastic wrap is purified… and it will drip slowly into the smaller bowl.

Not sure you trust this method? Try "contaminating" some clean water in the larger bowl with salt and food coloring. The condensation you collect will be clear and un-salty.

RadarScope
radarscope.tv
If you're stuck in the house on a stormy day, you can virtually chase severe weather such as tornados using the latest technology.

Bee Friendly
waitrose.com/bees
Help researchers at the University of Sussex in England understand which bushes and flowers in your garden attract the most bees by collecting and uploading your observations.

Solve the Outbreak
**cdc.gov/mobile/
Applications/STO**
Want to play disease detective? This tablet app from the Centers for Disease Control and Prevention lets you decipher data and solve medical puzzles as you play epidemiologist to track down the source of mysterious outbreaks.

Earth-Now
jpl.nasa.gov/apps/
Using this NASA app, check out the earth's vital signs: air temperature, sea level, carbon dioxide levels, even ozone levels.

Merlin
merlin.allaboutbirds.org
Identify any feathered friend you happen to encounter—based on its size, color, and location. You can also learn more about birds' behaviors and even listen to their songs.

INSTANT ADVENTURE

READ THE
CLOUDS

Clouds are formed of water or ice droplets so light and tiny that they float in the air. Besides being beautiful to look at, you can use their formations to forecast the weather.

LOW CLOUDS Below 6,500 Feet

Cumulus
Shaped like cotton balls with flat bases. These clouds can be as low as 3,300 feet above ground. If they are widely spaced, expect good weather.

Cumulus Congestus
A cumulus cloud with a top that looks like the head of a cauliflower. Can predict either good or bad weather, depending on if they turn into...

Cumulonimbus
Sometimes the top looks more like an anvil—which means lightning, thunder, snow, hail, heavy rain, even tornadoes.

Stratus
Look like fog but don't touch the ground. These gray clouds can produce drizzle—but usually don't mean rain.

Nimbostratus
Dark gray, these thick clouds cover the entire sky and produce light rain and snow.

IS IT A CLOUD?

Contrails
Vapor trails from airplanes, created when the humid air evaporating from the jet mixes with the extremely cold air way up there.

Illustrations by Mister Reusch

MIDDLE CLOUDS Between 6,500 and 23,000 Feet

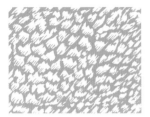

Altocumulus
If you spot these on a humid summer morning, it's likely there will be thunderstorms later in the day.

Altostratus
Gray clouds that usually blanket the entire sky. They signal that storms are coming.

Altostratus Undulatus
They look like ripples on a pond. They signal that a change in weather is on the way.

HIGH CLOUDS Above 23,000 feet and higher

Cirrus
They get their feathery shapes from high winds. Cirrus clouds usually mean the weather will change within 24 hours.

Cirrostratus
Sheetlike clouds so thin you can see the sun or moon through them. They often appear 12 to 24 hours before it rains or snows.

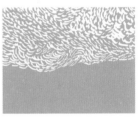

Cirrocumulus
These white puffs look like scales on a fish. They indicate fair but cold weather; however, in tropical regions, they can signal hurricanes.

SPECIAL CLOUDS

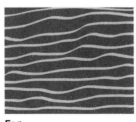

Fog
A cloud that touches the ground. It usually means the next day will be fair.

Lenticular
Shaped like flying saucers, they are created by mountain wind patterns. They signal increasing winds and storms.

Virga
Streaks of rain or snow that hang beneath a cloud. They produce thunder and lightning.

CLOUDSPOTTING
& WAVE WATCHING
Q&A with Gavin Pretor-Pinney

Gavin Pretor-Pinney is founder of the Cloud Appreciation Society, which boasts thousands of members.

His book *The Cloudspotters's Guide* examines the science, history, and culture of clouds. And *The Wave Watcher's Companion* introduces us to waves of all kinds—from ocean waves to light waves and shock waves. In order to predict the weather and navigate without high-tech equipment, an adventurer needs to be able to "read" clouds and waves. So we asked Pretor-Pinney for some tips.

UNBORED: Most of us already know that cloud-spotting is relaxing. But you claim that cloud-spotting is a useful activity, too. How so?

PRETOR-PINNEY: We've lost the ability to read the clouds… which is a shame. For one thing, we don't always have access to weather forecasts on TV or the Internet. For another, reading the clouds is a great way to connect to our surroundings. When you're out in nature, you shouldn't think of yourself as being *beneath* the sky—you're *in* it!

UNBORED: There are a lot of folk sayings about what certain types of clouds indicate, when it comes to predicting the weather. Is there any accuracy to these sayings?

PRETOR-PINNEY: My daughters know a cloud-spotting rhyme that's accurate: "In the morning, mountains; in the afternoon, fountains." On a sunny morning, if you notice cumulus clouds—the low, detached, puffy ones—developing vertically in rising mounds and growing tall in the sky, then it's quite likely to rain.

Photo courtesy Diana Muir

Illustrations by Mister Reusch

UNBORED: Then there's "Red sky at night, sailors' delight; red sky in the morning, sailors take warning." What does it mean when a cloud is painted red by the sun?

PRETOR-PINNEY: In temperate regions of the globe, weather tends to move from west to east. In the morning, if there are clouds above you but the skies are clear in the east where the sun is rising, then the sun's rays will color the underside of the clouds red. This is a sign that the clear weather has passed over you already, and a new weather front—possibly stormy—is heading in from the west. Red-painted clouds at sunset suggest that although there may be clouds above you right at that moment, the skies to the west—from which direction new weather will soon be headed your way—are clear.

UNBORED: Can you explain how the seafaring inhabitants of the South Sea Islands encountered by Captain Cook in the 18th century used clouds for navigation purposes?

PRETOR-PINNEY: In a tropical region you get a lot of water vapor, which is an invisible gas, floating above the sea's surface. When the vapor encounters an island, the warm air rising from the island's sun-heated surface kicks the vapor up higher into the atmosphere. As the vapor rises, it expands, and as it expands it cools off. Under the proper conditions, some of that cooled vapor condenses into droplets… and that's what a cloud is, a collection of countless tiny water droplets. So South Sea Islanders out at sea would navigate towards a cumulus cloud—which served as a beacon in the sky.

Red clouds in the morning mean that new, possibly stormy, weather is coming.

UNBORED: South Sea Islanders also studied waves for navigation purposes. How?

PRETOR-PINNEY: It's amazing that the human brain, when confronted by a confusion of waves, is able to focus on only those waves that are important to us. When you're having a conversation with a friend in a noisy place, although your ears are being bombarded with a cacophony of sound waves, you're able to pay attention to only those sound waves coming from your friend's mouth. South Sea islanders studied waves so carefully—they created beautiful stick charts called *mattang*— that they were able to distinguish which particular swells were "reflected" off an island, and which weren't. They used that knowledge to hold their direction while canoeing from island to island.

UNBORED: Might understanding how waves break on the shore save a swimmer's life?

PRETOR-PINNEY: When waves erode a channel into the seabed near shore, a rip current—which pulls water back from the shore and through the channel into deep water—can get set up. If you find yourself being swept out to sea, remember that the rip current only flows out where the channels have been hollowed in the seabed. So don't exhaust yourself trying to swim to shore within the rip current. Instead, swim steadily *parallel* to the

South Sea islanders created wave charts out of sticks and shells.

shoreline, and hopefully you will soon move out of the channel. A gap in the line of the breaking waves is sometimes an indicator of a rip current's position— because waves don't break where the water is deeper, as is the case over a rip current's channel. This, I guess, is a case of how wave knowledge can save your life.

UNBORED: Why are clouds and waves important to would-be adventurers?

PRETOR-PINNEY: They're not just worthwhile for intrepid navigation or forecasting! Clouds and waves, because they're eternally forming and expiring, put your life into perspective—and they remind you to live it to the fullest. As the American naturalist and philosopher Henry David Thoreau put it, while observing clouds one evening, "I see a city… in whose streets no traveller has trod… some Salamanca of the imagination." Salamanca, an ancient city in Spain, was a destination for adventurers—and what Thoreau suggests is that clouds are an invitation to an adventure of the imagination.

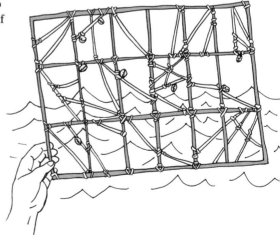

ADVENTURE SONGS

Exploring nature can involve camping together for days at a time. Here are a few songs to help you get through.

Don't know the tunes? Look the songs up on YouTube, or just make up your own. Traditionally, sailors and explorers would make up new verses—so you should, too.

Canoe Song

Canoers use this Canadian folk song to keep time while paddling. Can be sung as a round.

> My paddle's keen and bright
> Flashing like silver
> Follow the wild goose flight
> Dip, dip, and swing.
>
> Dip, dip, and swing 'er back
> Flashing like silver
> Swift as the wild goose flies
> Dip, dip, and swing.

Repeat these two verses, then:

> Dip, dip, and swing
> Dip, dip, and swing.

Blow the Man Down

Sea shanties were traditionally sung by sailors to help them work in unison on large merchant vessels. Each sailor would take a turn singing a solo verse, then all would join in on the chorus. Here's the most famous shanty. Make up a new verse related to your own adventure!

> I'll sing you a song, a good song of the sea
> Way-hey, blow the man down
> I trust that you'll join in the chorus with me
> Give me some time to blow the man down.

All sing the chorus:

> Blow the man down, bully, blow
> the man down
> Way-hey, blow the man down
> Blow the man down, boys, from
> Liverpool town
> Give me some time to blow the
> man down.

Here's a sample verse:

> As I was a-walking down Paradise
> Street
> Way-hey, blow the man down
> A handsome young damsel I
> happened to meet
> Give me some time to blow the
> man down.

All sing the chorus.

Captain James T. Kirk

"The Grand Old Duke of York" is a classic campfire song. Thanks to the popularity of the 1960s TV show *Star Trek*, in recent years this "Grand Old Duke" parody has become a new campfire classic. Want to turn it into a game? Eliminate players who get the actions wrong.

> Oh, Captain James T. Kirk
> He had four hundred men
> He'd beam them up to the *Enterprise*
> And down to the planet again.

Stand when singing "you're up," and sit when singing "you're down." When singing "beaming up," wave your arms sinuously. When singing the final line, stand at "up" and sit at "down."

> When you're beamed up, you're UP
> When you're beamed down, you're
> DOWN
> But when you're stuck while
> BEAMING UP
> You're neither UP nor DOWN.

Repeat these two verses at increasingly fast tempos. When you're ready to end the song, substitute the following verse. When you sing "red shirt," put your hands up to your head in distress. When you sing "around," first throw your hands up defensively, then collapse.

> When you're beamed up, you're UP
> When you're beamed down, you're
> DOWN
> But when you wear a RED SHIRT
> You soon won't be AROUND.

R.I.P., Leonard Nimoy, 1931–2015.

BAKE BREAD
ON A STICK

Bannock is a dense, quick bread that is a lot like a scone. Campers and outdoor adventurers know that when you wrap bannock dough around a stick and cook it over a campfire, it's an easy and delicious treat.

> **CAUTION!** When building a campfire or baking over one, grownup supervision is a must.

You'll need:

- 1 cup flour
- 1 teaspoon baking powder
- ¼ teaspoon salt
- 2 tablespoons powdered milk
- 1 tablespoon oil or melted butter
- Water
- Mixing bowl
- Large resealable plastic bag
- Sticks suitable for campfire cooking
- Camping knife (use with grownup supervision)
- **Optional**: Honey, cinnamon, sugar, jam, more butter

Illustrations by Mister Reusch

Make the bannock dough

1. While you are still at home, whisk the flour, baking powder, salt, and powdered milk together in a bowl. (This recipe makes four servings, so if you want more bannock you'll have to double the ingredients listed.) Seal the mixture of dry ingredients inside the plastic bag. (Figure A)

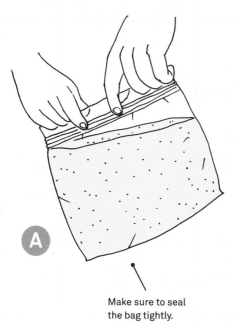

Make sure to seal the bag tightly.

2. At the campsite, empty the bag of dry ingredients into your mixing bowl. (Figure B) Add the oil or butter to the mixture, and knead it together: It will be dry and crumbly. Then add some water, a tiny amount at a time, until the mixture feels like Play-Doh. It shouldn't be sticky.

Find a stick

1. Find sticks suitable for campfire cooking. Green twigs fresh off the tree are best, but if you are in an area that prohibits gathering green wood, then look for sticks on the ground that are still strong. Try to use a stick that's approximately the width of two of your fingers.

2. Use the camping knife to strip the bark from one end of the stick. Be careful, and always remember to cut away from yourself.

3. Temper your stick by holding it over the campfire until it becomes hot. Doing so will help the bannock cook from the inside as well as the outside. But don't burn the stick, or else that's how your bannock will taste.

Bake the bannock

1. Rolling a small portion of the bannock dough between your palms, form it into a snake shape. Wrap the dough in a downward spiral around the stripped end of your stick. The dough should be roughly ½" thick. (Figure C)

2. When the coals in your campfire are hot, hold the bannock over the coals—not too close! (Figure D) When the bannock starts to turn golden-brown, like a marshmallow, turn it. The bannock will get fluffier as it cooks. In about 10 minutes, it should be golden-brown on all sides.

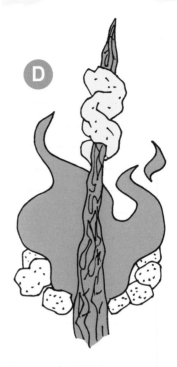

3. Slide the bannock off the stick—without burning your fingers—and eat it while it's warm. If you choose, you can slather the bannock in honey or jam; or roll it in a mixture of cinnamon, butter, and sugar; or just add more butter.

CAUTION! Extinguish the fire thoroughly before you leave it for the night by soaking the coals with water. Turn rocks in on the firebed. Feel the ashes to make sure the fire is completely cold. And if you're leaving the campsite, dismantle your stove and shovel the removed dirt back in.

BEST EVER

ADVENTURE MOVIES

I don't even exercise!

In our first book, **UNBORED**, we only had space to list a handful of favorite outdoor adventure movies—like *Little Fugitive, Captains Courageous, Around the World in 80 Days, Watership Down, The Black Stallion, Never Cry Wolf,* and *Soul Surfer.* Here is a more complete list.

1922
NANOOK OF THE NORTH

Directed by Robert J. Flaherty
An Inuit family travel across treacherous wintry terrain, hunt a walrus, and build an igloo—using traditional methods—in this docudrama shot in the Canadian Arctic. Though the scenes presented as reality were staged, the film's situations were more or less authentic; and viewers were impressed by the ingenuity, tenacity, and optimism of the protagonists, "Nanook" (whose actual name was Allakariallak) and his family.

1925
THE GOLD RUSH

Directed by Charlie Chaplin
In this adventure set in the Yukon territory of north-western Canada, during the Klondike Gold Rush of the late 1890s, the great silent film actor Charlie Chaplin plays a bumbling but plucky prospector. The scenes in which he and his bear-like friend, Big Jim, survive a blizzard—and are nearly blown off a cliff, in their cabin—are thrilling and also hilarious.

1937
HEIDI

Directed by Allan Dwan
Child star Shirley Temple plays a sweet-natured Swiss orphan who is sent to live with her reclusive grandfather in an Alpine hut on a remote mountaintop. Heidi learns to love the rural way of life—and she melts her grandfather's icy heart in the process. When she is kidnapped, Heidi's grandfather comes to the rescue. There is a sleigh chase!

Illustration by Mister Reusch

1938

THE ADVENTURES OF ROBIN HOOD

Directed by Michael Curtiz and William Keighley

The English folklore legend of Robin Hood, a wronged noble-man living as an outlaw in Nottinghamshire's Sherwood Forest, has been adapted as a movie many times… but the 1938 version remains our favorite. When you see Erroll Flynn (as Robin Hood) swing down from a tree branch, or fight Little John on a log over a river, you'll understand why.

1951

THE AFRICAN QUEEN

Directed by John Huston

As World War I breaks out, German soldiers in East Africa burn down the village where a prim-and-proper English missionary, Rose, has been working. Rose persuades Charlie, a rough-and-ready Canadian boat captain, to navigate his boat, *The African Queen*, to a large lake downriver… where they'll attempt to blow up a German gunboat. But first they must survive dangerous rapids and a leech-filled swamp!

1963

THE INCREDIBLE JOURNEY

Directed by Fletcher Markle

Left behind when their owners go on a trip, two dogs (a young Labrador Retriever and an old Bull Terrier) travel 250 miles—through the sparsely populated wilderness of northern Canada—in search of their beloved masters. They're accompanied by an unlikely comrade: a Siamese cat. Together, they face bears, a rushing river, and more.

1972

THE COWBOYS

Directed by Mark Rydell

Rancher Wil Andersen (played by cowboy actor John Wayne) needs replacement drovers for a cattle drive, but none are available… except for a group of schoolboys. Can they learn to rope, brand, and herd cattle? More importantly, how will they react when Andersen is bushwhacked by rustlers? Critics at the time didn't appreciate the violent scenes; but the boys' use of craft and guile against the rustlers is impressive. So is Wayne's tough advice, to his young students, to show up every day "with grit teeth."

1972

SOUNDER

Directed by Martin Ritt

In rural Louisiana, a loving and strong family of African American sharecroppers nearly starves during the Depression. When his father is sent to prison for trying to steal food, 11-year-old David sets out on a personal odyssey—through the state's back roads—to visit him. He is accompanied only by his father's injured but devoted dog, Sounder.

1987

THE PRINCESS BRIDE

Directed by Rob Reiner

There are many things to love about this movie: the fencing master Inigo Montoya, who seeks revenge on the man who killed his father; the enormous and kind-hearted Fezzik; the sword-fighting. But Buttercup and Westley's ordeal in the Fire Swamp, where they face fire spouts and Rodents of Unusual Size, is a terrific adventure in its own right.

2008

PONYO

Directed by Hayao Miyazaki

This lovely animated movie is about Ponyo, a fish-girl who lives beneath the waves, and her new friend Sôsuke, a five-year-old human boy. Ponyo wants to become human—so her sea-goddess grandmother tests them by flooding the land with water. Sôsuke and Ponyo must rescue Sosuke's mother.

2009

FANTASTIC MR. FOX

Directed by Wes Anderson

When Mr. Fox, a retired poultry thief, and his opossum friend steal food from three farmers (Boggis, Bunce, and Bean), his home gets destroyed and his nephew is captured. What to do now? This stop-motion adaptation of Roald Dahl's children's novel is rated PG (for action, smoking, and slang humor) but it's innocent fun.

SINK OR SWIM

AN EXCERPT FROM

THE BLACK ARROW

by Robert Louis Stevenson

Joanna Sedley, the heroine of the 1888 historical adventure *The Black Arrow*, is also one of its heroes. How so? When the book's protagonist, Dick Shelton, first meets her, she is disguised as a boy and going by the alias of Jack Matcham. Dick (who'd been engaged to marry Joanna, though the two had never met, before Joanna rejected him) doesn't think that girls are handy when it comes to adventure. However, when he falls into a river, and "Jack Matcham" comes to the rescue, he learns that he's mistaken.

"Stand, Dick Shelton!" bawled the man upon the island. "Ye shall have no hurt, upon the rood! Stand! Back out, Hugh Ferryman."

Dick cried a taunting answer.

"Nay, then, ye shall go afoot," returned the man; and he let drive an arrow.

The horse, struck by the shaft, lashed out in agony and terror; the boat capsized, and the next moment all were struggling in the eddies of the river.

When Dick came up, he was within a yard of the bank; and before his eyes were clear, his hand had closed on something firm and strong that instantly began to drag him forward. It was the riding-rod, that Matcham, crawling forth upon an overhanging willow, had opportunely thrust into his grasp.

"By the mass!" cried Dick, as he was helped ashore, "that makes a life I owe you. I swim like a cannon-ball." And he turned instantly towards the island.

Midway over, Hugh Ferryman was swimming with his upturned boat, while John-a-Fenne, furious at the ill-fortune of his shot, bawled to him to hurry.

"Come, Jack," said Shelton, "run for it! Ere Hugh can hale his barge across, or the pair of 'em can get it righted, we may be out of cry."

And adding example to his words, he began to run, dodging among the willows, and in marshy places leaping from tussock to tussock. He had no time to look for his direction; all he could do was to turn his back upon the river, and put all his heart to running.

Presently, however, the ground began to rise, which showed him he was still in the right way, and soon after they came forth upon a slope of solid turf, where elms began to mingle with the willows.

But here Matcham, who had been dragging far into the rear, threw himself fairly down.

"Leave me, Dick!" he cried, pantingly; "I can no more."

Dick turned, and came back to where his companion lay.

"Nay, Jack, leave thee!" he cried. "That were a knave's trick, to be sure, when ye risked a shot and a ducking, ay, and a drowning too, to save my life. Drowning, in sooth; for why I did not pull you in along with me, the saints alone can tell!"

"Nay," said Matcham, "I would 'a' saved us both, good Dick, for I can swim."

"Can ye so?" cried Dick, with open eyes. It was the one manly accomplishment of which he was himself incapable. In the order of the things that he admired, next to having killed a man in single fight came swimming. "Well," he said, "here is a lesson to despise no man. I promised to care for you as far as Holywood, and, by the rood, Jack, y' are more capable to care for me."

"Well, Dick, we're friends now," said Matcham.

DANGER!

Exploring nature is fun. But be careful out there! Here's how.

BEASTS & BUGS

You should never approach a **black bear,** no matter how cute. And never get between a bear and her cub. When camping, store your food in lockers outside your tent.

Deer ticks can be carriers of Lyme disease. Walk in the center of a trail, away from grass and brush; tuck your pants into your socks; and shower after a hike, if possible.

Although not dangerous, a **leech** is definitely gross. Use your fingernails to break the seal of its mouth on your skin... this should cause the leech to loosen its jaws.

You can spot a **brown recluse spider** by the violin-shaped marking on its back... and the fact that it has six eyes. This spider's bite can be extremely painful.

While most **mosquito** bites are just a nuisance, these bugs can sometimes carry serious viruses. Protect yourself by wearing long pants and sleeves, particularly at dusk.

PLANTS

The sap of **poison ivy** contains urushiol, an oily allergen that can cause an itchy rash and blisters if it touches your skin. Remember this rhyme: "Leaves of three, let it be."

The leaves of **poison oak,** which come in clusters of three, may resemble those of oak trees... but this plant is a close relative of poison ivy, so avoid it.

Stinging nettles are covered with tiny hairs that sting like mad. Remove them by putting a piece of tape over the affected area... then yanking it off.

Illustrations by Mister Reusch

WATER

Why is it harder to swim in a river than in a pool? Because of strong **currents**. Don't swim where two rivers come together—currents are often unpredictable in these spots.

A **sneaker wave** is a large wave that can sneak up and pull you into deep water. When you're in the water at the beach or the shore, never turn your back on the surf.

Hypothermia occurs when your body temperature gets dangerously low and can't return to normal. When it's freezing cold, dress in layers and always wear a hat.

WEATHER

Giardia is a water parasite that causes severe diarrhea. Never drink water from lakes, rivers, or streams unless it's been purified.

An **avalanche** is a fast and unexpected flow of snow down a hill. Don't ski, snowboard, or snowshoe in backcountry areas that haven't been groomed.

If you get caught in a storm and there are **lightning strikes,** don't take shelter under a tree. Instead, crouch down and keep your head low—without letting it touch the ground.

Rip currents are strong channels of water in the ocean that pull you from the shore out over your head. Swim steadily parallel to the shore until you're out of it.

Dehydration can be life-threatening if it's severe enough. So if your mouth gets dry and sticky, or if you are having a tough time urinating, it's time for a water break.

Besides being painful, a severe **sunburn** can cause skin cancer. Always apply sunscreen before you head out on your adventure, and wear a hat with a brim.

contraband
Master in the
hideout

←10→

Forbidden
Zone

smugglers'
contraband

confiscated
contraband

Referee

Contraband pits bold
Smugglers against
the Forbidden Zone's
vigilant Patrol.

MASSIVE
OUTDOOR
GAMES

Do you live near a large park with trees, boulders, bushes, and other features?

Round up a crowd of friends and family, and play these adventure games. They're fun for all ages, and as darkness falls they only get more exciting and awesome.

CONTRABAND

Adventurers: The more the merrier

You'll need:

- A referee who will also serve as timekeeper
- Bandannas, colored t-shirts, or some other way to differentiate teams
- Smuggler's contraband, in the form of (for example) 25 slips of paper: 10 marked "50"; 5 marked "75"; 5 marked "100"; 4 marked "150"; and 1 marked "500." You could also use Monopoly money, poker chips of different colors, playing cards, or other objects.

Try this:

1. Agree on the playing field's boundaries. Within these boundaries, you'll need a 10'x10' space to serve as the Forbidden Zone, as well as a small Hideout (from which the Contraband Master will send Smugglers). Agree on a time limit: 20 minutes is good. Divide into two teams: the Smugglers and the Patrol. The Smugglers should choose one of their teammates to be Contraband Master, who will remain in the Hideout all game.

2. Before the game begins, the referee should move into the Forbidden Zone. The Contraband Master should distribute contraband to various Smugglers. Be strategic: Slower Smugglers, acting as decoys, might carry low-value contraband, while faster Smugglers—following the decoys—carry high-value contraband. Don't distribute all the contraband right away; Smugglers should return throughout the game to pick up more.

The Contraband Master not only distributes contraband, but strategizes a plan.

Contraband Master's Hideout

3. The referee announces "Game on!" and starts the clock. The Patrol fans out, in an attempt to tag any Smuggler approaching the Forbidden Zone. Smugglers attempt to sneak or rush into the Forbidden Zone without getting tagged. If successful, a Smuggler delivers the contraband to the referee, then returns to the Hideout for more.

4. Here are some suggested rules for smuggling, and for searching detained smugglers. The contraband can only be concealed in your pocket, in your hand, or under your hat; no hiding contraband in your shoes or under your clothes.

If a Smuggler is tagged by a member of the Patrol, then he must stand still and count to 30 aloud while the Patrol searches his pockets, hands, and hat. After 30 seconds, the Smuggler is free to go.

5. Any contraband confiscated by the Patrol is turned over to the referee. The referee should keep the two piles of contraband separate. Once the time is up, the referee should tally up the the total value of each pile of contraband—and announce a winner.

If captured, a Smuggler can be frisked for up to 30 seconds.

The object of Posse is to capture as many flags as possible.

GAME ON!

extra flags

Referee in Neutral Zone

POSSE

Adventurers: The more the merrier

You'll need:

- A referee who will also serve as timekeeper
- A pencil or pen and paper for the referee, for keeping score
- A large flag for each of the two teams—each team must choose a color. You can use a sweatshirt, pillowcase, etc., as long as it's in that team's color.
- Several small flags for each player. You can use bandannas, torn-up shirts, etc., as long as they're in that team's color. They should be large enough to wear tied onto your head.
- Two medium-sized flags for each team's captain, in their respective team's colors

Try this:

1. Agree on the playing field's boundaries, including the referee's Neutral Zone somewhere near the middle of the playing area. Agree on the time limit: Half an hour, say. Agree that the big flag counts for 50 points, the team captain's flag for 25 points, and each small flag for 3 points.

2. Divide into two teams, and select a captain for each team. During the game, some members of each team should travel with the captain in order to protect them.

3. Divvy up the small flags: one per player. Each player tucks a small flag into their waistband, except for the team captains—who wear the medium-sized flags tied onto their heads.

If your flag is captured, you can rejoin the game later.

4. The referee should take all the leftover small flags, as well as her pencil, pen, and watch, and move into the Neutral Zone.

5. At the start of the game, each team has a few minutes to hide their flags. You'll know when to start and stop when the referee yells "Go!" and "Time's up!" As in Capture the Flag, the idea is to put it somewhere visible but inconvenient; it should not be thrown high into a tree, say, or buried.

6. When the referee yells, "Game on!" the game begins. The object is to capture the other team's big flag and as many of their small flags as you can—while protecting your own team's big flag and your own small flag. Captured flags should be given to the referee, who will keep a running tally of points earned by each team and redistribute the flags as necessary.

7. If your flag is captured, you must walk—not run—to the referee and be issued a new one. No one is ever out of the game; you can always rejoin.

8. If one team captures the other team's big flag, then the game ends. If neither team captures the other team's big flag, then the game ends when the time runs out. Once the game ends, the referee adds up each team's points and announces the winning team. Note that it's possible for a team to win even if their large flag was captured!

HOT STUFF!
COOK OVER A FIRE PIT

Nothing tastes so good as food that you've prepared on an open fire. Often, that's because you're hungry after a day of outdoor activities. But it's also because cooking over an open fire is the most fun way to prepare a meal.

These recipes are perfect for car camping, or cooking on a backyard fire pit… which we'll tell you how to build.

CAUTION! When building or cooking over a campfire, grownup supervision is a must. Extinguish the fire thoroughly before you leave it for the night by soaking the coals with water. Turn rocks in on the firebed. Feel the ashes to make sure the fire is completely cold. And if you're leaving the campsite, dismantle your stove and shovel the removed dirt back in.

BUILD YOUR
FIRE PIT

Find a site where there's little chance of a fire spreading: if possible, a sheltered space where the ground is sandy or rocky.

You'll need:

- Large rocks for the fire's perimeter; and a large flat rock, for the fire's "chimney."
- Dry wood. You'll need both kindling and larger pieces. All the firewood should be approximately the same size—so the fire will burn down evenly. You want an even heat, and no flames scorching your food and your cookware.
- Newspaper or other tinder
- A large container of water, for dousing the fire
- Shovel or trowel
- A metal cooking grid; you can borrow one from your backyard gas grill.
- Matches or lighter
- **Optional:** Hatchet, for splitting firewood into kindling. Use with grownup supervision.

Try this:

1. Using the shovel or trowel, scrape away 1–2" of soil where your stove will be.

2. Lick a finger and hold it up to test the direction of the wind. Your wet finger will feel colder when it's pointed directly at the oncoming breeze.

3. Using large rocks, construct a U-shaped stove. Place the large, flat "chimney rock" at the rear of the stove; it will help direct smoke up and away. Have the rear of the stove face the

wind. (Figure A) (How wide should your stove be? Your metal cooking grid ought to be supported by the stove's two sides.) Fill in gaps with smaller rocks.

4. Make sure that your cooking grid sits firmly and evenly atop the stove. Then place it to the side. (Figure B)

5. Lay down a layer of crumpled sheets of newspaper, or other tinder, in the fire pit. Stack several layers of kindling over the tinder, alternating direction with each layer. (Figure C) Do not construct a campfire-style pyramid of kindling; this is a cooking fire!

6. Set the bucket of water near the fire pit. But not right next to it.

7. Light the tinder. (Figure D) When the kindling is ablaze, distribute a layer of firewood evenly over the entire fire bed. (Figure E & F) You want it to burn evenly. IMPORTANT: Make sure to use enough firewood not only to cook your meal, but to ensure that the embers are still hot enough to cook dessert while you're enjoying your dinner.

8. Don't cook over flames—you'll burn the outside of the food before the inside is done! As soon as the flames die down, use a stick to rake the coals into a higher level at the back end of the fire pit, leaving just a thin layer of coals at the front. Place cooking grid onto the stove, at the back end. You now have two cooking areas: the grid, for food that requires a lot of heat; and the thin layer of coals.

GET
COOKING

The following recipes feed 6 people. Start cooking the potatoes and corn first—they take longer.

Cooking gear

- Mixing bowls (or large zip-lock bags)
- Kitchen knife
- Meat-safe cutting board (not wood)
- Long-handled grill spatula, fork, and tongs
- Wooden spoon
- Oven mitt or hot pad
- Can opener
- Heavy-duty aluminum foil

APPETIZERS

GRILLED ASPARAGUS

Even kids who don't like asparagus think it tastes amazing when grilled. And it makes your pee smell different.

You'll need:

- One bunch of asparagus
- Marinade: 2-3 tablespoons olive oil, salt, and pepper

Try this:

1. Wash the asparagus, and trim about ½" to 1" off the tough cut ends.

2. Toss asparagus with olive oil. Salt and pepper to taste. Don't like pepper? When you're cooking over an open flame, pepper becomes less spicy.

3. With the cooking grid over the less hot section of your fire, spread the asparagus evenly on the grid.

4. Cook, turning frequently, until asparagus is lightly seared and soft.

SKILLET NACHOS

Who needs a microwave? This cheesy appetizer is *muy delicioso.*

You'll need:

- A bag of corn chips
- Grated cheese; we prefer Monterey Jack.
- A jar of salsa
- Cast iron skillet
- Heavy-duty aluminum foil
- **Optional:** A can of black beans

Try this:

1. Distribute a layer or two of chips in the skillet, and sprinkle cheese over it. Repeat.

2. If you're adding the black beans, go ahead and add them now.

3. Add more chips and cheese.

4. Cover the nachos with aluminum foil, to trap heat inside. (Figure A)

5. Place skillet onto cooking grate. Cook until cheese melts.

6. Remove skillet from heat, remove aluminum foil, and add salsa. You can eat them right out of the skillet—just be careful not to touch it while it's hot.

MAIN COURSE

CHICKEN SHISH KEBAB

According to tradition, the shish kebab ("kebab" is Persian for "frying"; "shish" is Turkish for "skewer") was invented by medieval Turkish or Persian soldiers who used their swords to grill lamb's or goat's meat over open fires. Chop, marinade, skewer, and cook—what could be simpler?

You'll need:

- Approx. 2 lbs. of chicken breast cut into 1" cubes
- Two red or yellow onions, cut into quarters
- Two red or green peppers, cut into eight sections apiece
- Marinade: ¼ cup olive oil, 2 cloves of thin-sliced garlic, a lemon, salt and pepper to taste
- Metal skewers
- Meat thermometer
- **Optional:** 1 teaspoon dry oregano
- **Optional:** Whole cherry tomatoes, whole mushrooms

Try this:

1. Combine olive oil, sliced garlic, salt and pepper (oregano, if you choose) and toss in mixing bowl with cubes of chicken. Cover and let marinate in refrigerator or cooler for 1 to 3 hours.

2. Half an hour prior to grilling, add lemon juice and toss again.

3. Just prior to grilling, slip the chicken and vegetables onto skewers. Try a skewer with 2–3 pieces of pepper, then 4–5 pieces of chicken, then cap it with 2–3 pieces of onion. This is because the coals are hotter in the center of the stove than at the edges, and meat requires more heat than veggies do.

4. Place kebabs directly onto the cooking grate for 15–20 minutes until done. Keep an eye on them, rotating until each side has been seared the same amount. Make sure the chicken is cooked thoroughly to 165 degrees on the thermometer.

HOBO CORN

Wrapped in foil and heated over a fire, corn on the cob will steam itself.

You'll need:

- 6–12 shucked ears of corn
- A yellow onion, sliced thin
- 1 tsp. butter or olive oil, per ear of corn
- Salt and pepper, to taste
- 6–12 sheets of aluminum foil, each 10"–12" long

Try this:

1. Place each ear of corn in the middle of a sheet of aluminum foil. Form the foil into a bowl around the corn.

2. Add a couple of onion slices, the butter or olive oil, and salt and pepper.

3. Close the aluminum foil bowl and wrap it tightly around the corn.

4. Cook wrapped ears of corn on the cooking grid for 15–20 minutes. You'll hear it sizzling. Check on it after 10 minutes or so, to make sure it's not burning.

CAMPFIRE POTATOES

Hot potato! Or should we say, hot potatoes. Either way, they're delicious.

You'll need:

- 6 large baking potatoes (or any potatoes), washed and sliced into ¼"-thick pieces
- A yellow onion, sliced thin
- 1–2 tsp. butter or olive oil, per potato
- Salt and pepper, to taste
- A sheet of heavyweight aluminum foil (or two sheets of normal foil), 24" long

Try this:

1. In center of aluminum foil sheet, pile the potato and onion slices in a few layers. Form the foil into a bowl shape around the potatoes and onions.

2. Top with butter or oil, and salt and pepper.

3. Close the aluminum foil bowl and wrap it tightly around the potatoes and onions.

4. Cook wrapped potatoes and onions on the cooking grid for 15–20 minutes. You'll hear it sizzling. Check on it after 10 minutes or so, to make sure it's not burning.

BANANA
MELTS

Prepare this dessert ahead of time. Then, while you're eating dinner, toss these packets directly into the embers.

You'll need:

- 6 unpeeled bananas
- A bag of chocolate chips
- 6 sheets of tinfoil, each 10"–12" long
- **Optional**: peanut butter chips or butterscotch chips

Try this:

1. Using your kitchen knife, make a vertical slice in each banana—don't cut it in half, and don't cut all the way through—to create a "canoe" shape.

2. Place each banana onto a sheet of tinfoil. Form the tinfoil into a bowl shape around the banana.

3. Stuff chocolate chips into the banana's opening. Close the tinfoil bowl and wrap it tightly around the banana.

4. Cook wrapped bananas directly in the fire's embers, for 15 minutes or so—until the chips are melted and the banana is squishy. Don't worry about burning your dessert, because the banana skins offer lots of protection.

c1000 Gudrid Thorbjarnardottir, known as the "Far Traveler," sails west from Greenland off the edge of the known world—along with a crew of Vikings seeking Leif Eriksson's fabled Vinland.

1766–1769 Frenchwoman Jeanne Baret disguises herself as a man in order to join a French expedition sailing around the world. She becomes the first woman ever to circumnavigate the globe.

1804–1806 Sacagawea, a teenage Native American from the Shoshone tribe, acts as an interpreter and guide on the Lewis and Clark expedition across the Western half of the United States.

A Secret History

1889–1890 Determined to beat the fictional record set in Jules Verne's novel AROUND THE WORLD IN EIGHTY DAYS, American journalist Nellie Bly circumnavigates the globe in just over 72 days.

1906 American mountaineer Fanny Bullock Workman sets an altitude record for women when she scales Pinnacle Peak —nearly 23,000 feet above sea level—in the Himalayas.

1925 After being excluded from the National Geographic Society, America's greatest female explorer, Harriet Chalmers Adams, helps launch the Society of Women Geographers.

1932 American aviator Amelia Earhart becomes the first woman to fly solo nonstop across the Atlantic. In 1937, while attempting to fly around the globe, she and her plane disappear.

1963 Russian factory worker and skydiver Valentina Tereshkova pilots the spacecraft Vostok 6, becoming both the first woman and the first civilian to fly in space.

1975 Despite being nearly killed in an avalanche, Japanese mountain climber Junko Tabei becomes the first woman to reach the summit of Mount Everest.

# of Female Explorers

1986 Marine biologist Sylvia Earle ties the world solo dive depth record in a submarine— and sets the record, for women, when she descends to 1,000 meters in a sub she helped design.

2001 School teachers turned explorers Ann Bancroft and Liv Arnesen become the first women to sail and ski across Antarctica—completing a trek of nearly 100 days.

2012 After fighting the Dutch courts, which thought she wasn't old enough, 16-year-old Dutch sailor Laura Dekker becomes the youngest person to circumnavigate the globe single-handed.

Avoid snow blindness!

MAKE
SNOW GOGGLES

On a bright winter day, sunlight reflected from ice and snow can make your eyes hurt—a lot.

In order to prevent the painful condition known as snow blindness while sledding, skiing, or snowshoeing, you should wear sunglasses. Traditionally, the Inuit people of the Arctic made their own ivory or wood *ilgaak* (snow goggles), which featured narrow viewing slits. Inspired by *ilgaak*, here's a duct tape craft project that just might spare your eyeballs from a sunburn.

Illustrations by Heather Kasunick

You'll need:

- Duct tape
- Scissors
- Tape measure
- Pen
- Enough string to go more than halfway around your head

Try this:

1. Cut four 7" lengths of duct tape. If the distance between your two temples is much more or less than 7", you might want to cut the lengths of duct tape to a more precise measurement. Place the four lengths of duct tape on your work surface, sticky sides facing up.

2. Place the first strip of duct tape on top of the second, lengthwise, with a ¼" overlap between the top of one strip and the bottom of the other. Both pieces of tape should be sticky side up.

3. Now place a third strip of duct tape, sticky side down, on top of the first (which is sticky side up). Finally, place the fourth strip, sticky side down, on top of the second (also sticky side up). There should be a ¼" overlap between the bottom of the third strip and the top of the fourth. You've created a double-thickness duct-tape rectangle.

4. Trim away any sticky bits from the edges of your rectangle, then—using the tape measure—find the midpoint of the rectangle's bottom (long) edge. Cut out a triangle, at that midpoint, for your nose.

5. The tape just above the top point of the triangle you've cut is the "nose bridge" of your goggles. On either side of the nose bridge, you'll want to cut thin slits for seeing through. Using the tape measure, determine the distance between the bridge of your nose and the center of one of your eyes. From the center of the goggles' nose bridge, measure that same distance to the left and mark the spot with a pen. Next, measure that same distance to the right of the goggles' nose bridge and mark the spot.

6. Fold the rectangle lengthwise, so that the marked spots are on the folded edge. At each marked spot, cut a very thin horizontal slit—no more than ¼" high and 1" wide.

7. Using one blade of the scissors, punch a hole at each end of the snow goggles. Tie a double knot at one end of your length of string, and thread the string through one of the punched holes. Thread the unknotted end through the second hole, and tie another double knot.

GO OUTSIDE!

Is your grownup a couch potato who isn't convinced that getting you outside is important?

Sunlight and fresh air are healthy and relaxing. Research has demonstrated that kids who spend lots of time outdoors are less anxious (and therefore better at concentrating—on schoolwork, say) than those who spend their time indoors. So train your grownup to get you out of the house!

> **IMPORTANT!** Should your grownups join you in your outdoor adventures? Sometimes, certainly. But they should also let you explore on your own.

Tell stories

Last Child in the Woods author Richard Louv suggests that you ask your grownup to tell you stories about what he or she liked doing outdoors, when he or she was your age. Back in those days, kids spent a lot more time outdoors than they do now. You may be amazed to hear about your grownup's adventures in the woods, in vacant lots, in parks, and out in the street. Hearing about this mostly unsupervised outdoor fun may give you some ideas for what you'd like to do outdoors… and it will help you understand why it bothers grownups to see you spend a beautiful day indoors watching TV, playing videogames, or staring at a computer screen.

Illustration by Mister Reusch

Go for a Green Hour

Do you feel cranky and anxious if you spend a lot of time indoors? Experts agree that you need to be outdoors for at least an hour each day, which is why the National Wildlife Federation recommends that your grownup build a "green hour" into your family's daily schedule. As soon as you get home from school—after you eat a snack, and before you have any screen time—spend 60 minutes outside with your siblings and friends.

We promise you won't run out of ideas for what to do, but here are a few activities to get you started: ride your bike, skateboard or scooter, shoot hoops or play street hockey, rake leaves, photograph tree bark or graffiti, plant and tend a vegetable or flower garden, walk the dog, throw snowballs, run through the sprinkler (unless there's a drought), larp, throw a frisbee or baseball, play hide-and-seek, jump rope. For lots more ideas, check out our book *UNBORED Games*.

Head for the hills

Many kids spend at least part of their weekend playing club soccer or volleyball, taking dance (or music, or karate, or math) lessons, or doing something else that's organized by grownups. These sorts of activities can be great—but it's also important for you and your family to get out into nature together. So convince your grownup to commit to at least one unorganized outdoor outing per weekend. It doesn't have to last all day, it shouldn't involve special gear, and it should be free. The National Wildlife Foundation's Nature Find app (nwf.org/NatureFind.aspx) will direct you to parks, forests, natural areas, reservations, wildlife sanctuaries, orchards, and farms near you.

Dig the dark

After the sun goes down, don't go indoors… and ask yourself the following questions. What unusual sounds do you hear? How does the air feel on your skin? Can you name the moon's phase? Can you see any constellations? If you're camping out, how far can you and your grownups walk without using a flashlight—just navigating by the light of the moon?

Get in gear

Rain and snow are no excuse to stay indoors—just ask any kid who lives in Seattle or St. Paul. Unless there's lightning, or the temperature is below freezing, go ahead with your daily green hour and your weekend family outings. Just make sure that you have the proper outdoor garb. If you live in a winter climate, that means a jacket, snowpants, boots, mittens, hat, long underwear, and a scarf or face mask. (Add toe and hand warmers, if it's really cold.) For the rest of the year, a rain jacket and rain boots will do the trick. On sunny days, no matter what the temperature, don't forget to wear sunscreen and a brimmed hat to protect your skin.

Untame your yard

Turn your yard into a place where wildlife can thrive. Build a birdhouse and feeders. Install a birdbath. Attract pollinating insects—including bees and butterflies—by growing asters, buckwheat, coneflowers, coreopsis, goldenrods, ironweed, Joe-weed, and sunflowers. Harvest the seeds from these flowers to provide food for winter birds and other wildlife. Visit the Audubon Society's Healthy Yards website (athome.audubon.org/yard) for more ideas like these.

EXPLORE THE NIGHT SKY

Betelgeuse

Orion

Taurus

Canis Major

Sirius

Memorizing the shape and location of these northern-hemisphere constellations and stars is a great way to explore the night sky— perhaps from your own backyard.

Big Dipper
Look north and it's easy to spot this ladle-shaped constellation. In summer it shines high in the sky. In winter, it hovers near the horizon.

North Star/Polaris
While other stars' apparent positions in the sky change throughout the night, the North Star doesn't budge.

Little Dipper
Easiest to spot in a moonless country sky because a few of its stars are quite dim. Polaris is the outermost star on the handle.

Cassiopeia
From Polaris, trace an imaginary line in the opposite direction of the Big Dipper. You'll hit a "W"- or "M"-shaped clump of stars.

Illustrations by Mister Reusch

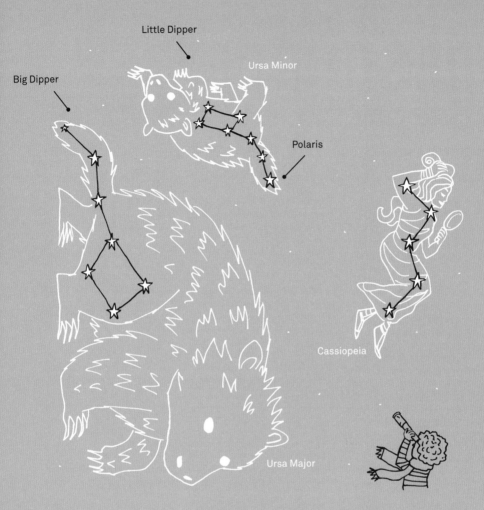

Big Dipper

Little Dipper

Ursa Minor

Polaris

Cassiopeia

Ursa Major

Orion
Easiest to spot in winter. Look south toward the horizon and you'll see a giant tilted hourglass. Midway down, the line of three bright stars forms Orion's belt.

Orion Nebula
A curved line of stars hangs from Orion's belt—that's his scabbard. Halfway down the scabbard, you'll see a glowing ball of dust. Amazing when seen through a telescope.

Betelgeuse
A bright orange star that's found at the upper left of Orion, marking the right arm. This is a red supergiant—a star nearing the end of its life.

Sirius
Using the stars of Orion's belt, trace a path downward from east to west and you'll find the brightest star in the evening sky.

Taurus
Follow an imaginary line up Orion's belt from west to east. Taurus the bull is the "V" with one very bright star.

PS: You can also use an app to search for constellations— we like Star Walk.

RESOURCES

Adventure-ize

Airliners.net. Not only does this extensive website include photographs of all planes currently flying, but you can enter the tail number of a plane that you're about to board and see where else it has traveled around the world.

Cockpit Confidential (2013), by Patrick Smith. The author, an airline pilot and adventurous world traveler, offers answers to every question—from how flight works to turbulence to airport security—that you might have about flying, airplanes, airports, and the global airline industry. There's more info at his website: AskThePilot.com

Cool Tools: A Catalog of Possibilities (2013), by Kevin Kelly. Gadgets and gear useful for everything from long-distance bike rides to natural disasters, reviewed by adventurous types who've tried them out.
Also check out the website: kk.org/cooltools.

Fifty Dangerous Things (You Should Let Your Children Do) (2011), by Gever Tulley and Julie Spiegler. Drive a car! Play in a hailstorm! Break glass! Lick a battery! You get the idea. We also recommend the authors' inspiring website, tinkeringschool.com.

Free to Learn (2013), by Peter Gray. Common-sense wisdom from a developmental psychologist, who argues that giving kids the freedom to pursue their own interests through play will make them happier, more self-reliant, and better students for life.

Hitchhiker's Guide to the Galaxy, The (1979), by Douglas Adams. This science fiction adventure is satirical... but you'd be surprised at how many real-life adventurers claim it's one of their favorite books. Its central message is very good advice: "Don't panic."

How to Do Nothing with Nobody All Alone by Yourself (1958, 2010), by Robert Paul Smith. An amazing book of kid lore—with info about how to make your own toys out of everyday objects; and how to amuse yourself endlessly.

How to Stay Alive in The Woods: A Complete Guide to Food, Shelter, and Preservation Anywhere (1956, 2001), by Bradford Angier. Learn how to build a shelter, catch game without a gun, plus other survival tips we hope you won't ever need.

Lost Art of Finding Our Way, The (2013), by John Edward Huth. Throughout history, humankind has discovered and invented amazing navigational strategies and tools. Though written for grownups, this book raises questions—about our reliance on GPS, for example—that the whole family will enjoy discussing.

RedCross.org. Search by state to find a swimming and water safety class near you, not to mention courses on First Aid, CPR, emergency planning, and other life-saving skills.

Strange Maps (2009), by Frank Jacobs. An atlas of 100+ "cartographic curiosities" mapping everything from imaginary lands, to the *Apollo 11* and *Apollo 12* moon walks. Curated by the editor of the always astonishing Strange Maps blog at BigThink.com.

Worst-Case Scenario Survival Handbook, The (1999), by Joshua Piven. Everything you need to know in case you ever need to land a plane, wrestle an alligator, or get inside a moving train.

You Are Here: Personal Geographies and Other Maps of the Imagination (2003), by Katharine Harmon. Gorgeous and creative maps of people's towns, cities, states of minds, and more. Your grownup may call this an "art book." We just think it's awesome.

RESOURCES

Adventures Close to Home

Acorn Pancakes, Dandelion Salad, and 38 Other Wild Recipes (1995), by Jean Craighead George. Yummy recipes for foragers, from the author of the YA adventure novels *My Side of the Mountain* (1959) and *Julie of the Wolves* (1972).

Alvin's Secret Code (1963, 2015), by Clifford B. Hicks. Not only is this an exciting adventure, it's an engaging primer on cryptography—which is to say, writing and cracking codes. The author was an editor of the magazine *Popular Mechanics* who really knew his stuff.

Backyard Ballistics (2nd edition, 2012), by William Gurstelle. Potato cannons! Paper match rockets! Fire kites! By the author of the equally imagination-sparking book *Defending Your Castle: Build Catapults, Crossbows, Moats, Bulletproof Shields, and More Defensive Devices to Fend Off the Invading Hordes* (2014).

Backyard Foraging (2013), by Ellen Zachos. A field guide to over 60 familiar plants—greens, fruits, nuts, seeds, tubers, and fungi—you didn't know you could eat. The author explains how to identify, harvest, and prepare each plant... carefully.

BenandBirdy.blogspot.com. Catherine Newman, who has contributed to two UNBORED books (so far), publishes an entertaining blog about her family's obsessions—one of which is cooking and eating adventurously. Here you'll find delicious recipes that the whole family will love... along with some brilliant writing.

Crafting with Paracord (2014), by Chad Poole. Paracord, a lightweight nylon kernmantle rope, is supposedly the world's strongest cord. This book demonstrates 50 paracord craft projects—including durable bracelets and knife grips. Cool!

Fix It, Make It, Grow It, Bake It: The D.I.Y. Guide to the Good Life (2010), by Billee Sharp. Every kind of around-the-house adventure you can imagine. From kitchen cures to seed-sharing, to making your own cleansers.

Geek Dad (2010), by Ken Denmead. We're fans of the blog GeekDad.com, and this spinoff is crammed with DIY projects, including pirate cartography and nighttime kite flying. We also dig the book's two sequels: *The Geek Dad's Guide to Weekend Fun* (2011) and *The Geek Dad Book for Aspiring Mad Scientists* (2011). Not just for dads.

Geek Mom (2012), by Natania Barron, Kathy Ceceri, Corrina Lawson, Jenny Williams. GeekMom.com is a terrific family activity blog, and we enjoy how this spinoff challenges us to see daily life as an adventure waiting to happen. Projects include: creating a secret lair, topology tricks, and capturing wild sourdough yeast. Not just for moms.

Kids' Places to Play (2004), by Jeanne Huber. How-to instructions—for grownups and kids—on building treehouses and other play structures. Plus: A spider web climbing net! A periscope! A climbing wall! A bicycle roller coaster!

Playborhood (2012), by Mike Lanza. Grownups often complain that kids don't play in the street as much as they used to. Lanza not only diagnosed the problem, he created solutions in his own neighborhood. You'll find an interview with the author in this book. You can also follow him on Twitter: @playborhood

SnowDayCalculator.com. Based on the severity of the weather in your zip code, and the strictness of your school district, this website offers precise predictions as to how likely it is that tomorrow will be a snow day. It was invented by a middle-schooler!

RESOURCES

Urban Adventure

Adventurous Book of Outdoor Games, The (2008), by Scott Strother. Your Internet-deprived grownups grew up playing street and playground games like Bombardment, Cops and Robbers, Kick the Can, and Wall Ball. Here are the rules.

AtlasObscura.com A user-created guide to the world's most amazing and unusual places—some far away, and some right in (or near) your own town. You'll find an interview with the site's founders, Joshua Foer and Dylan Thuras, in this book.

Bicycle!: A Repair & Maintenance Manifesto (2013), by Sam Tracy. The author, who for many years worked as a mechanic in Minneapolis bike shops, aims to provide bicyclists with the know-how to take simple bicycle repairs into their own hands. Topics include essential tools, on-the-road repairs, scavenging, locks, and preventing rust.

Bike Snob (2010), by BikeSnobNYC. The author, also known as UNBORED contributor Eben Weiss, mocks aspects of hipster bike culture while celebrating the joys of bicycling. Also check out his blog, Bike Snob

NYC (bikesnobnyc.blogspot.com), and his other books, *The Enlightened Cyclist* (2012) and *Bike Snob Abroad* (2013).

Everyday Bicycling: How to Ride a Bike for Transportation (2012), by Elly Blue. Advice for how to make biking an adventure that can also improve our health, the environment, and our community. You'll find an interview with the author in this book. Also check out Blue's wise and witty blog, Taking The Lane (TakingTheLane.com).

Free-Range Kids: How to Raise Safe, Self-Reliant Children (Without Going Nuts with Worry) (2010), by Lenore Skenazy. Do your grownups have a hard time letting you out of their sight, much less explore the city? Urge them to check out this book, the author's website (FreeRangeKids.com), and her Twitter feed (@freerangekids).

Handmade Skateboard, The (2014), by Matt Berger. A skateboard is a tool of liberation. This book demonstrates to you and your grownup everything you need to know to design and build a custom longboard, cruiser, or street deck from scratch.

Imaginary World of..., The (2014), by Keri Smith. Unlike most grownups who want kids to tear themselves away from

screens and go outdoors, the author of this book (not to mention *How to Be An Explorer of the World*) makes doing so really fun and exciting.

Life Skills for Kids: Equipping Your Child for the Real World (2000), by Christine M. Field. A homeschooler offers lessons on everything from using a check book to boiling an egg, to doing the laundry and reading a map.

Pay It Forward Movement (payitforwardmovement.org). Do a favor for another person. What's expected is that the recipient of the favor will do the same for others. This website is full of ideas for ways you can be helpful... while having a social adventure, too.

Transit Maps of the World (2007), by Mark Ovenden. If you didn't think you needed a subway or light rail map of every city in the world, this book will prove you wrong.

WorldCarfree.net. This website is the hub of the global "carfree" movement, which seeks to revitalize towns and cities, and create a sustainable future. Each September 22, this group organizes World Carfree Day; check out the website for events near you.

Our favorite adventure books, websites, and more

RESOURCES

Nature Adventure

Be Out There (NWF.org/Be-Out-There.aspx). Type your zip code into this website's NatureFind app and you'll be pointed in the direction of great nature spots within a hundred miles. You'll also find lots of ideas about how to have fun outdoors.

Book of Totally Irresponsible Science: 64 Daring Experiments for Young Scientists, The (2008), by Sean Connolly. This book is just what it sounds like.

Cabinet of Curiosities (2015), by Gordon Grice. From devil's claws to carrion beetles, this book is packed with fascinating weirdness. It's perfect for kids and grownups who love to collect stuff in nature... and then bring that stuff home and display it.

Camp Out!: The Ultimate Kids' Guide (2007), by Lynn Brunelle. A charming book that's less about how to camp out than about how to have fun doing so. Campfire songs, cookout recipes, information about constellations and animal tracks, outdoor games, ghost stories... you name it.

Cloudspotters Guide, The (2007) by Gavin Pretor-Prinney. "Life would be immeasurably poorer without clouds," claims Pretor-Prinney. We agree!

You'll find an interview with the author in this book. Also check out *The Cloud Collector's Handbook* (2011) and the Cloud Appreciation Society website (CloudAppreciationSociety.org).

Complete Walker IV, The (2002), by Colin Fletcher and Chip Rawlins. Absolutely everything you'll ever need to know to be an expert backpacker.

Kitchen Science Lab for Kids: 52 Family Friendly Experiments from Around the House (2014), by Liz Lee Heinecke. Super cool activities you can make at home, including spy juice, nature walk bracelets, and a shoebox solar viewer. For more activities (and how-to videos), check out kitchenpantryscientist.com.

Last Child in the Woods: Saving Our Children from Nature-Deficit Disorder (2005), by Richard Louv. This book, which reminds us why it's important to get outside and spend time in nature, is already a classic. Follow the author on Twitter: @RichLouv

Medicine for Mountaineering & Other Wilderness Activities (2010), by James A. Wilkerson. This book goes way beyond what you learn in a first aid class to help you deal with minor to life-threatening injuries when you're unable to get help quickly.

Mountaineering: The Freedom of the Hills (8th Edition), by The Mountaineers and Ronald C. Eng. In print and continually updated for over 50 years, this classic explores all aspects of climbing and mountaineering, from basic knots to serious peak ascents. Also check out their essential gear recommendations: mountaineers.org/learn/how-tos/the-ten-essentials

National Geographic Society (adventure.nationalgeographic.com/adventure). Gear tips, adventure news, and photos from the international authority on exploration. Plus: trip ideas, national parks, and more.

National Outdoor Leadership School's Wilderness Guide, The (1999), by Mark Harvey. A how-to book for backpacking and other outdoor adventures, including mountaineering, kayaking, and sailboat travel.

Wave Watcher's Companion, The (2010), by Gavin Pretor-Pinney. Everything you'd ever want to know about what the author calls "life's undulations," from ocean waves to light waves to shock waves... and even unnatural phenomena like stadium waves!

INDEX

TEAM UNBORED

Joshua Glenn is a semiotic analyst, editor of HiLobrow.com, and coauthor of several books, including *The Idler's Glossary* and *Significant Objects*. He has worked as a newspaper, magazine, and website editor; and he was the "Brainiac" columnist for *The Boston Globe*. He used to publish the zine/journal *Hermenaut*. He lives in Boston with his wife and two sons.

Heather Kasunick teaches visual arts in a public high school. She has exhibited at the Brattleboro Museum and Art Center, the Fitchburg Museum of Art, and The MPG Contemporary Gallery (Boston), among other venues. She lives in Northampton, Mass., with her husband and their dog. More info: wondercupboard.blogspot.com

Elizabeth Foy Larsen is a writer and editor whose stories on children and families have appeared in *The New York Times*, *Mother Jones*, *Parents*, and *Slate*. She has worked as a newspaper, magazine, and website editor. In the 1990s, she was a member of the team that launched *Sassy*, a magazine for teen girls. She lives in Minneapolis with her husband, daughter, and two sons.

Tony Leone is principal of Leone Design, a graphic design studio and consultancy in Boston. His work has been honored by the American Institute of Graphic Arts, and has been featured in *Communication Arts*, *Print*, *Graphis*, and elsewhere. During the 1990s he was the art director of *Hermenaut*. He lives in Boston with his wife, son, and daughter. More info: leone-design.com

Chris Piascik is an illustrator residing in Massachusetts. Since 2007, he has been posting daily drawings to his website; in 2012, he self-published a book, *1000 Days of Drawing*. When he is not drawing weird pictures for the likes of Nike, McDonald's, and Red Bull, he teaches design at the University of Hartford. More info: chrispiascik.com

Mister Reusch has made illustrations for many different clients, including Burton Snowboards, StrideRite, and dog rescue groups. He teaches illustration at Massachusetts College of Art & Design in Boston and exhibits his paintings regularly in galleries. He lives in Haverhill, Mass., with his girlfriend and their dogs. More info: misterreusch.com

GO, DESIGN TEAM! Our book *Unbored: The Essential Field Guide to Serious Fun* won three prestigious design awards: *Print* magazine's Regional Design Annual, *HOW* magazine's International Design Annual, and the AIGA's Best of New England (BoNE) Show.

CONTRIBUTORS

Liz Lee Heinecke, author of *Kitchen Science Lab for Kids*, has gone from working at a lab bench to mixing up experiments with her kids. Via her website KitchenPantryScientist.com, her iPhone app KidScience (kidscienceapp.com), and frequent TV appearances, she demonstrates how families can do science at home.

Catherine Newman is the author of the book *Waiting for Birdy* and the blog Ben & Birdy. She writes for *FamilyFun* and other magazines, and edits the nonprofit kids' cooking magazine *ChopChop*. She lives with Ben, 15, Birdy, 12, Craney Crow, 6 (feline), and their dad in Amherst, Mass. More info: BenandBirdy.blogspot.com

Chris Spurgeon works at Patagonia. He is a computer programmer; a student of the histories of science, geography, cartography, and navigation; and a tinkerer who makes electronic gadgets and high-powered rockets. An avid traveler and outdoorsman, his favorite types of weather include hail storms, thunderstorms, and graupel (look it up).

Eben Weiss, otherwise known as "Bike Snob NYC," is a cyclist, blogger, and author of the books *Bike Snob: Systematically & Mercilessly Realigning the World of Cycling*, *The Enlightened Cyclist*, and *Bike Snob Abroad*. He lives with his family in New York City. More info: bikesnobnyc.blogspot.com

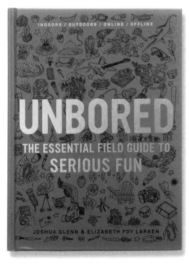

STAY
UNBORED

"It's a book! It's a guide! It's a way of life!"
— *Los Angeles* magazine

"If you can't find an exciting activity to do
in this book, there might be something
wrong with you."
— *Sports Illustrated Kids*

"Loaded with projects, games, experiments
and just plain fun."
— *MAKE* magazine

"Be creative, try new things, figure out
how things and systems work, and just
maybe change the world in the process."
— *Parents & Kids Magazine*

UNBORED is more than just adventure. Get the guides that started it all!
Both the original UNBORED and UNBORED GAMES are packed with activities—from
crafts and DIY projects to games you can do with your friends and family.

Available wherever books are sold.

Make sure you also check out our seriously fun MindWare activity kits, including
UNBORED Disguises and UNBORED Treasure Hunt.

UNBORED | U.S. $28.00 / CAN. $34.00 | ISBN: 978-1-60819-641-8
UNBORED GAMES | U.S. $16.00 / CAN. $19.00 | ISBN: 978-1-62040-706-6

Bloomsbury.com | **Unbored.net**

790.1922   Glenn, Joshua,
GLE   1967-

          Unbored adventure.

          MAY 0 9 2016